ON THE CLOCK

ON THE CLOCK

The Story of the NFL Draft

BARRY WILNER AND KEN RAPPOPORT

TAYLOR TRADE PUBLISHING
Lanham • Boulder • New York • London

Published by Taylor Trade Publishing
An imprint of The Rowman & Littlefield Publishing Group, Inc.
4501 Forbes Boulevard, Suite 200, Lanham, Maryland 20706
www.rowman.com

Unit A, Whitacre Mews, 26-34 Stannary Street, London SE11 4AB, United
Kingdom

Distributed by NATIONAL BOOK NETWORK

British Library Cataloguing in Publication Information Available

Library of Congress Cataloging-in-Publication Data
Wilner, Barry.
  On the clock : the story of the NFL draft / Barry Wilner and Ken
Rappoport.
    pages cm
  ISBN 978-1-63076-101-1 (pbk. : alk. paper) — ISBN 978-1-63076-102-8
(electronic) 1. Football draft—United States. 2. Football players—United
States—Recruiting. 3. National Football League. I. Rappoport, Ken. II.
Title.
  GV954.32.W57 2015
  796.330973—dc23
                                                                    2014042789

∞™ The paper used in this publication meets the minimum requirements of
American National Standard for Information Sciences—Permanence of Paper
for Printed Library Materials, ANSI/NISO Z39.48-1992.

Printed in the United States of America

CONTENTS

PROLOGUE

The National Football League (NFL) draft features no action on the field. No passing, running, tackling, or kicking. Hey, there isn't even a field. Yet the draft has become more popular than many other sporting events, including the National Basketball Association (NBA) and the National Hockey League (NHL) playoff games, against which it goes head-to-head for viewers. In fact, the draft has spawned its own cottage industry in which names such as Gil Brandt, Mel Kiper Jr., and Mike Mayock become as well known as any of the first-round selections.

In *On the Clock*, we chronicle the history of the proceedings. As veteran sportswriters, we take you from the first grab bag in 1936, when Philadelphia chose Heisman Trophy winner Jay Berwanger of the University of Chicago and saw him decline to play in the NFL, to the 2014 draft—considered one of the deepest in talent ever.

Along the 78-year journey, learn about the competitions for the top overall spot (Peyton Manning versus Ryan Leaf), the unhappy No. 1s (John Elway and Tom Cousineau), the big flops (JaMarcus Russell), and the late-rounders-turned-superstars (Tom Brady).

Meet the draft wizards, from Paul Brown to Bill Walsh and Jimmy Johnson. And the draft whiffs that cost personnel executives their jobs.

On the Clock takes you behind the scenes at one of pro football's yearly major events.

ACKNOWLEDGMENTS

We would like to thank the following for their help with *On the Clock*:

Howard Balzer, Upton Bell, Chris Berman, Gil Brandt, Sean Butler, Simmi Buttar, Steve Cohen, Bill Fitts, Andrew Fitzpatrick, Dave Goldberg, Bill Hofheimer, Mel Kiper Jr., Pat Kirwan, Joe Linta, Jim Lippincott, Alex Marvez, Mike Mayock, Brian McCarthy, Paul Montella, Nick Pavlatos, Alex Riethmiller, Ralph Russo, Adam Schein, Michael Signora, Allison Stoneberg, John Wildhack, Charlie Yook, and Jon Zimmer.

1

DRAFT DAY 2014

The Most Exciting Draft Ever

A red carpet laid out along a midtown Manhattan street, leading directly into Radio City Music Hall. The perfect setting for Jay-Z and Beyoncé. Or Miranda Lambert and Blake Shelton.

Not so much for the young men strolling along it in their $1,000 designer suits, cameras following their every stride. Ask any one of them, from Jadeveon Clowney to Johnny Manziel, and their preference might be a green field, in the uniform of an NFL team.

Alas, the NFL draft went Hollywood years before Clowney, Manziel, and Michael Sam headlined the strongest and most intriguing class of prospects in years, perhaps ever. The pomp and primping is all part of the show now—a show that, for an event that involves no final score and, basically, no real sports action, has become a monster hit.

"The increased popularity of the draft has been phenomenal," NFL commissioner Roger Goodell said. "We think our fans look at it as a significant part of our year, just as they do our games and the Super Bowl."

More fans than ever looked at the 2014 draft, drawing record viewership for NFL Network and ESPN, which cotelevised the proceedings. (That two networks would devote a pair of nights and a Saturday afternoon to the draft speaks as loudly as Mel Kiper Jr. espousing the virtues of Blake Bortles as a pocket passer.)

And no draft in the previous 78 years had quite the cachet.

First, there was the quantity: with a record 102 early entrants—including South Carolina defensive end Clowney and Texas A&M quarterback Manziel—more collegians than ever were available for plucking.

Of course, quantity only matters when counting up Lombardi Trophies in a team's collection. And for quality, 2014's crop was so rich that many NFL teams felt they could strike it rich, with picks deep into the draft, and pick up bargains.

Ramping up the drama was the NFL's decision to move the draft back two weeks, ostensibly because Radio City would not be available in late April due to a special spring spectacular. Turns out, the show was not so spectacular and wound up being canceled, but the league had already set its schedule for 2014.

One league executive even confided anonymously, "If this works, and we are pretty sure it will, the draft is going to stay in May. It keeps it on people's minds for a longer time, and the buildup gets crazier and crazier the longer people are thinking and talking about it."

One topic fans (and, to a much larger degree, the broadcast media) couldn't seem to stop talking about was Sam, the first openly gay player in an NFL draft.

The presence of a gay player in the NFL should hardly have been news in 2014. Former All-Pro defensive back Troy Vincent, now the league's director of football operations—Goodell's right-hand man—said he played with at least a half-dozen gay players in the NFL.

"It worked, we won many football games," Vincent said. "They were players, and we didn't see them any differently."

Wade Smith played 11 pro seasons, albeit never revealing his sexual orientation. He is now an activist for gay rights, and Goodell invited Smith to speak to team owners at the league's annual meeting six weeks before the draft.

Goodell recognized how sensitive the issue could become in the buildup to the draft. "I found his message to be very important for all of us to hear," Goodell said of Smith. "He's part of the family that we all are in the NFL. He just wants to make sure we provide that workplace where people can go and play football and be comfortable playing."

Sam himself echoed Goodell's (and Smith's) words. He asked to be judged solely by his on-field credentials, as hundreds of other players would be. He had no criminal record or nonfootball problems. No major injuries to concern NFL team doctors.

Hell, he was the Southeastern Conference's (SEC) Defensive Player of the Year. Guess who else played in the SEC: Clowney, virtually a consensus top overall pick.

This was a draft that some preferred to turn into a societal statement. In the months after Sam made his announcement in February—directly after the Super Bowl, in fact—plentiful dialogue was devoted to Sam's sexuality, not his sacking skills. A distracted Sam's performances suffered, and a poor showing at the NFL combine, followed by an injured hamstring at his pro day, saw his stock plummet.

Even as the spotlight found its way to Sam, it never strayed very far from Clowney and Manziel. Their story lines, while not nearly as potent outside of the football community, for sure were the stuff of sporting soap operas.

While in high school at South Pointe in Rock Hill, South Carolina, Clowney was already attracting attention. Not just from the colleges, either, although he was the most highly recruited player in the nation; pro teams were enamored of his potential.

When Clowney declared for Steve Spurrier's Gamecocks, the entire state—outside of Clemson fans, naturally—rejoiced. Clowney would surely tear up the SEC and lead South Carolina to untold glory.

Clowney was one of the nation's best freshmen in 2011, and had he been eligible for the 2012 draft, he might have been chosen just behind quarterbacks Andrew Luck and Robert Griffin III.

In his sophomore season came his signature play, a hit on Michigan's Vincent Smith in the Outback Bowl that popped Smith's helmet as the player fumbled. Clowney grabbed the ball with one hand the way Godzilla grabbed cars off the street and devoured them.

The six-foot-six, 256-pound end was so dynamic in his second season as a Gamecock that he was almost unanimously considered college football's top prospect, a surefire No. 1 overall choice for the lucky team that finished at the bottom of the NFL standings.

Except, once again, Clowney was not eligible under NFL rules. He had to stay one more season at South Carolina.

And there was the rub. Clowney's performances in 2013 didn't soar off the charts; they plunged off them. His play was generally mediocre. At times he seemed disinterested. It was as if he was protecting himself from injury—and protecting himself for a big payday sure to come the following May when he could be drafted.

NFL scouts, general managers (GMs), and personnel directors took note, and suddenly the slam-dunk first pick was being slammed for his lack of work ethic, his selfishness, and his "uncoachability," as one analyst put it.

Just as suddenly, a debate as heated as the Peyton Manning–Tom Brady rivalry erupted about Clowney's value.

"To me, he is the No. 1 pick, whether it is to the Houston Texans or somebody else," analyst Kiper said, calling Clowney a "once-in-every-20-years talent. I don't see how you can take anybody over Clowney."

Ex-NFL running back Merril Hoge, now a TV commentator, didn't agree. He called Clowney an "atrocious football player." "Jadeveon Clowney does not play very smart as a football player. He has a long learning curve to be successful in the NFL."

Clowney called Hoge's remark "a spit in the face."

"I think I should be the No. 1 pick in the draft, definitely," he said. "I came out of high school as the No. 1 player, so I want to come out of here as the No. 1 guy."

Adding to all that intrigue was the "Johnny Football" (Manziel) factor.

The first freshman to win the Heisman Trophy, Manziel became a folk hero in Texas even before he collected the award. His reputation was firmly entrenched after leading the Aggies to a shocking upset of the defending national champion Crimson Tide in 2012.

That legend grew not only because of his spectacular play-making on the field—a combination of Fran Tarkenton, Doug Flutie, Drew Brees, and Houdini—but also thanks to Manziel's growing rep as a "playah" away from the gridiron.

He embraced all images of Johnny Football, adoring the attention for his Manziel Miracles in games and loving the limelight while hanging out with the beautiful people when not in uniform (or in school, for that matter).

"It's been life for so long now, I don't really know what it could be like any other way," Manziel said. "It's just how things are, wherever I want to go people are taking pictures and think I'm doing something wild when I'm just living a normal life."

Well, normal for a transcendent star, which anyone nicknamed Johnny Football has to be.

And like Clowney and Sam, there were plenty of doubters trying to offset the supporters as the draft drew near.

Was Manziel a franchise quarterback (QB)? Could his style, built more on instinct, footwork, and fearlessness than on the measurables the NFL seeks, successfully translate to the pros?

Would his lifestyle get in the way? Was a team getting Johnny Football the player or Johnny Famous the celebrity?

"Johnny's got the arm strength. He's got intelligence. He's got the wow factor," said draft analyst Mike Mayock in comparing Manziel to Hall of Famer Steve Young. "Now he's just got to learn to win by making some NFL throws from the pocket."

Begging to differ—big-time—was ESPN's Ron Jaworski, a quarterback who guided the Eagles to one Super Bowl appearance and might watch more game film than anyone on the planet.

"He's a random quarterback who likes to get out of the pocket and make plays with his legs," Jaworski told SiriusXM NFL Radio. "In the NFL, he won't last three games playing that style. He'll get hurt. He took a lot of vicious hits at A&M in the last two years. I wouldn't take him in the first three rounds."

The buildup over, the buzz in Radio City Music Hall as Goodell stepped to the podium to announce Houston's first pick was near deafening. The suspense in the green room where the prospects sat had already been snapped—Clowney had been informed by the Texans that he was the man. But the thousands of fans inside the Music Hall didn't know that.

With shouts of "John–ny, John–ny" and "Clown–ey, Clown–ey" drowning out each other, Goodell gave a quick smile and said, "With the first pick in the 2014 NFL draft, the Houston Texans select . . ."

As Goodell spoke Clowney's name, the defensive end began slapping hands with several other players. His eyes were moist as he hugged some of his peers and then headed out onto the stage to the kind of loud applause usually reserved for a pick by one of the New York teams. As Kiper, Mayock, and the NFL's longtime draft guru Gil Brandt all nodded their heads in acknowledgment of what they expected, Clowney vowed that unlike 12 years ago when the Texans took David Carr first overall and wound up with a flop, he was the real thing.

"I'm going to be something great," he said.

With Clowney off the board and on his way to teaming with 2012 Defensive Player of the Year J. J. Watt for what could become an unstoppable pair, Manziel took center stage.

Well, not exactly, considering he would remain in the green room seemingly forever while a score of other players—some of them not even on hand—would get the call from the "commish."

Still, Radio City rocked in anticipation of seeing Johnny Football grab the spotlight once more. Instead, the first quarterback off the board was Central Florida's Blake Bortles, whose stock surged late in the 2013 season and particularly in postseason workouts and interviews. Bortles also had the measurables (6–5, 230) that the just-under-six-foot, 205-pound Manziel lacked.

Jacksonville bit on Bortles at No. 3 overall, but the next team up was QB-poor Cleveland, a club that had openly courted Manziel for weeks. Just when the Manziel fans' eagerness was about to turn into frenzied expectation, the Browns traded the pick to Buffalo, which had drafted its QB of the future, EJ Manuel, the previous year.

Groans. Boos. Catcalls.

And this from a refugee from the Dawg Pound—yes, he was dressed in Browns garb and had a canine mask: "Noooooooo!!! WHAT ARE YOU DOING TO US?"

The Browns fans' frustration was palpable. It would grow exponentially a short while later.

The Bills jumped from ninth to grab Sammy Watkins. Clemson's star receiver would not have been a bad choice for Cleveland since the Browns had lost top wideout Josh Gordon for violating the league's drug policy.

While Dawg Pounders lamented a lost opportunity, Manziel's legions eagerly awaited three of the next four spots. Oakland, Tampa Bay, and Minnesota all seemed in the market for QBs, so surely their guy would get snagged by the Raiders, Buccaneers, or Vikings.

Or not. Manziel's name was not on the selection cards Goodell was handed for the Raiders and the Bucs.

But the Vikings were working the phones, looking to deal out of the eighth slot. And guess who dived in—albeit moving up just one place.

Cleveland. Surely to take Johnny Football.

That's what the "experts" thought. It's what the folks in the Radio City seats clamored for. It was a natural fit.

Ah, but these are the Browns. The object of their affection wasn't a QB at all—forget that the franchise hasn't found a winner at the position since returning to the NFL in 1999. It was Oklahoma State cornerback Justin Gilbert.

"The first defensive back of the draft goes, while Manziel still sits in the green room," NFL Network host Rich Eisen said, somewhat smugly as the audience exploded in derisive reaction.

Poor Gilbert was greeted with something less than adulation when he joined Goodell at the podium. Things were getting ugly in a hurry at the Music Hall.

The Manziel mania began overshadowing the machinations that saw the next 13 teams ignore quarterbacks. Not that the likes of the Lions, Giants, Bears, Steelers, Cowboys—despite Jerry Jones's proclaimed admiration for Johnny Football—Ravens, Saints, or Packers were really in the QB market.

By now, nearly three hours into the draft, the green room had emptied significantly. Manziel remained, with new nicknames such as "Johnny Freefall."

Manziel even got proactive, according to Browns quarterbacks coach Dowell Loggains.

"We're sitting there and they keep showing Johnny on TV, and Johnny and I are texting," Loggains said. "And he shoots me a text and he says, 'I wish you guys would come get me. Hurry up and draft me because I want to be there. I want to wreck this league together.' When I got that text, I forwarded it to the owner (Jimmy Haslam) and to the head coach (Mike Pettine). I'm like, 'This guy wants to be here. He wants to be part of it.' As soon as that happened, Mr. Haslam said, 'Pull the trigger. We're trading up to go get this guy.'"

Philadelphia owned the 22nd pick and had no interest in Manziel. The trigger, indeed, was pulled.

This time, the cognoscenti were certain, Manziel was Cleveland bound.

This time, they were right.

As Goodell approached the microphones, the "John–ny" chants were louder than ever. Browns fans on hand were woofing away.

"With the 22nd pick of the 2014 NFL draft, the Cleveland Browns select Johnny . . ."

No one could hear the last name. No one needed to hear it.

Manziel was on his cell phone talking to the team and at first had little reaction to the choice. Soon he smiled, exchanged hugs with his entourage, put his suit jacket back on, and then headed to the stage. He donned a Browns cap, held his hands above his head, and rubbed his fingers together in response to the cheers; he warmly embraced Goodell, and even patted the commissioner on the shoulder as if he had done something special.

"I like the fact Cleveland came back and got the young quarterback," shouted ESPN analyst Jon Gruden, who'd spent enough time in the off-season with Manziel to believe he was the real thing.

"I really, truly believe Cleveland was where I was supposed to wind up," Manziel said. "It feels right and feels like where it's meant to be."

He meant near Lake Erie, not sitting for hours waiting 22 picks to hear his name.

Manziel made the media rounds, each time denying he was ticked off by the long wait. At least that delay was hours, not days.

The controversial Sam, meanwhile, had to wait a while longer before joining the NFL. Sam, who did not attend the draft, nonetheless was never far away from the madding crowd at the Music Hall. His situation—or cause, depending on whom you were listening to—became the major focal point as the rounds progressed and the picks dwindled down.

With less than an hour left in the proceedings, and eight picks remaining, Sam had not been chosen. At the end of one of the most engaging selection meetings ever, the NFL appeared on the verge of a draft debacle.

As league executives contemplated how they could minimize Sam going undrafted—it's called damage control—and faced the even darker prospect of him not being signed as a college free agent by anyone, St. Louis Rams coach Jeff Fisher was speaking up in the team's war room.

The Rams hadn't seriously discussed picking Sam because, frankly, the defensive line might have been their strongest position. But with two consecutive selections, both compensatory picks that can't be traded, Fisher suggested to his bosses that they take Sam.

General Manager Les Snead and Rams CEO Kevin Demoff signed off immediately on the pick, but Fisher knew team owner Stan Kroenke would need to give the final OK—given the media circus that would follow Sam.

Fisher, one of the more progressive coaches and people in the NFL for nearly three decades, got the go-ahead and was soon on the phone with Sam. Sam's reaction when Fisher told him St. Louis, just a couple of hours from where he played college ball in Columbia, Missouri, was his destination? He broke down crying.

Why now and why the Rams?

"You know what, who knows? Only the people who sit in the war room know," Sam said. "They saw Michael Sam, day after day they scratched it off the board. That was their loss. But St. Louis kept me on that board."

Only a few dozen fans remained in Radio City, but when word filtered through the theater that Sam might be going to the Rams, the place became electric. And when NFL executive Mike Kensil strode to the podium—most of the picks on day 3 had been announced by team representatives, not by someone onstage—those folks in the audience began rhythmic clapping.

When Kensil spoke Sam's name, a loud cheer arose, followed by an immediate swiveling of heads toward the video screens above each side of the stage.

There was Sam, speaking on the phone but bent over, crying, his shoulders heaving. His boyfriend stroked Sam's arm, and when the phone call ended, they kissed, prompting responses ranging from support to outrage—at Radio City and everywhere else where his story had drawn observers.

"I know exactly what we're getting into, and I'm not worried at all," Fisher said.

Fisher couldn't have known everything the Rams were getting into. Such as Sam's representatives arranging with the Oprah Winfrey Network (OWN) to do a documentary on his attempt to make the NFL. St. Louis was blindsided by that one and, wisely, OWN and Sam's people decided to postpone production.

The Rams weren't pleased that such a distracting endeavor was even considered, but Fisher took it in stride.

"Michael Sam will help us," he said, "and we'll give him every chance to succeed, and you know what, it's going to be pretty cool."

Soon after, Memphis defensive back Lonnie Ballentine became the latest Mr. Irrelevant, chosen by Houston to close the grab-bag 255 picks after the Texans began it with Clowney. By then, the football appetite had been whetted for training camps 10 weeks away, to see if Clowney would be a dominator. If Manziel would be transcendent. If Sam would be a pioneer.

"And you know what, I feel like I'm a Clowney, a first draft pick," Sam said. "I'm proud of where I am now."

But Sam was released in the final preseason cut by the Rams, and wound up on the Dallas Cowboys' practice squad before being released after seven weeks. Still, he had gotten to the NFL, bringing the most extraordinary draft in football history to a headline-grabbing conclusion.

BENGALS DRAFT DAY

At 6:30 in the morning, Jim Lippincott, as usual, was about to begin his day. He checked phone messages and then called around the National Football League to see what was going on.

"You're still in the process of information gathering," said Lippincott, the Cincinnati Bengals' longtime director of football operations.

Yes, even on draft day, Lippincott was still chasing info. Like any of the other 31 NFL teams, the Bengals were trying to get a scouting report on what every team was thinking.

"You want to know what people were hearing about trades, people moving up, moving back," Lippincott said. "If you don't have a feel for what the other teams are going to do, you don't know whether to trade up or trade back."

"Maybe team A is interested in trading down, so they spend the morning of the draft calling around the league to see if anybody is interested."

As the chief scout for the Bengals for 20 years before his retirement from pro football, Lippincott worked his share of draft days. It never got old for him.

"It was an exciting time of year," Lippincott said. "From the scout's perspective, it was the culmination of 11 months of work."

The scouts' journey to the draft starts around Memorial Day when they receive the names of the available seniors from colleges around the country. The scouts would watch tape and begin to make travel plans.

Long before the time the NFL draft rolled around the following spring, the Bengals had made many decisions on the players they wanted.

In the draft room "things were going on, but we were never exchanging opinions because that work was already finished," Lippincott said. "In the 20 years I was there, there was never an argument."

Before draft day, it was time for the traditional mock draft.

"We would do the mock draft before we ranked the players regardless of position," Lippincott said.

"Each one of us had a team we were responsible for. Maybe I was responsible for the Pittsburgh Steelers. When the Steelers came up in our mock draft I would be an expert responsible for their needs and what they might do. Which means that maybe I would read the Pittsburgh *Post-Gazette*, maybe I would get on the phone and call [Steelers director of football operations] Kevin Colbert."

Not that a division rival would be all that forthcoming, but, well, information is vital at the draft.

"You had to know what the other team was doing. Otherwise, you don't know whether to trade up or trade back. If Sammy Sandwichmeat is your player, and you find out no one is interested in him, you can trade down, six, seven, eight spots, get the same guy and extra picks later in the draft."

Could be, too, that Sammy Sandwichmeat was coveted by two to three teams ahead of the Bengals.

"It will cost your team draft picks [to move up]. You have to be darn sure you know what you are doing. The lifeline of your team is draft picks, not free agency. Even the compensatory draft picks that show up at the end of different rounds are important to you. Draft picks are extremely important in putting together a football team. We have to be very careful in giving them away."

The Bengals' "War Room" was packed as the opening of the draft approached. Owners, coaches, scouts, medical staff. They sat around at tables shaped like footballs. In the front, owner Mike Brown and his brother, Pete, sat facing the assemblage.

"Everyone there had a function, everyone's opinion was needed," Lippincott explained.

The Bengals' roster, position by position, was displayed on a wall that had been painted with metallic paint. That allowed the Bengals to attach magnetic strips with players' names and schools.

The Bengals' board was divided in three categories: offense, prospects, defense.

At the 2014 draft, the Bengals had targeted the cornerback position as one of their biggest needs. They would pick 24th in the first round.

On the wall the board kept changing as picks were made by other teams, including cornerbacks.

The Bengals had ranked college players by position and then ranked all of them regardless of position.

"We had these players ranked, and as they disappeared, becoming members of other teams, we took the next highest on our board," Lippincott said, evoking the time-tested theory of sticking to your board regardless of circumstance.

Since Lippincott started with the Bengals two decades ago, things had changed dramatically in the war room. He remembers when there were old slate blackboards. He would get up there and put his "chicken scratch" on it. The security to protect the intelligence on the blackboard was an old canvas you pulled down like a Venetian blind to cover it up.

In 1992, when Lippincott was in his early days with the Bengals, all the work for the draft, including the mock draft, was done in one day.

"By the end of the day, everyone was so tired they couldn't think."

When coach Marvin Lewis joined the Bengals, he changed things. Lots of things.

The time devoted to the draft was exponentially expanded. The Bengals' day was divided so coaches also could work on football. They started earlier. "Everyone had a fresher mind," Lippincott noted.

Now, in the 2014 war room, the Bengals' turn had come. Everyone's attention was riveted on the magnetic board as they pondered their first-round choice.

The Bengals had watched as cornerback Justin Gilbert was selected by the Cleveland Browns at No. 8 and cornerback Kyle Fuller by the Chicago Bears at No. 14.

When the Browns moved up to No. 22 in a trade with Philadelphia to get Johnny Manziel, it was a slam dunk for the Bengals that the cornerback they coveted would be available. The Eagles, who needed a cornerback, were off the board.

At No. 24, the Bengals seized the opportunity. A unanimous first-team all American, Michigan State's Darqueze Dennard, was the choice.

"I thought he would probably be going in the middle of the draft," said Bengals defensive coordinator Paul Guenther. "It was a no-brainer at that point for us."

"Darqueze, are you ready to become a Bengal?" Lewis asked the five-foot-eleven, 202-pound Dennard in a phone conversation.

"Yes, sir."

TV analysts, as always, were giving their take on the picks. Talking about Dennard, former NFL linebacking great Ray Lewis said, "This is the type of corner Marvin Lewis loves. This kid loves a physical football game. And that's why when Marvin Lewis saw him still on the board he had to take him."

The Bengals selected eight players in all, four on offense and four on defense.

In the second round, the Bengals picked running back Jeremy Hill from Louisiana State University (LSU). There was some second-guessing about that choice, but Cincinnati liked Hill's combination of power and agility.

In the third round, it was Will Clarke, a defensive end from West Virginia. Coach Lewis felt Clarke, at six foot seven and 271 pounds, had the right dimensions for Cincinnati's aggressive defense.

In the fourth round, center Russell Bodine from North Carolina was chosen.

"Some of the best picks we made in my 20 years," said Lippincott, "were second, third, and fourth rounders—Carl Pickens, Darnay Scott, Corey Dillon—going back to the '90s."

Additional picks in the 2014 draft included quarterback A. J. McCarron from Alabama, linebacker Marquis Flowers from Arizona, wide receiver James Wright from LSU, and cornerback-safety

Lavelle Westbrooks from Georgia Southern. In addition, the Bengals later selected two compensatory picks.

There are time constraints in making every pick, of course; one team is always "on the clock." The team has 10 minutes to make its selection in the first round, then 7 minutes in round 2, and 5 minutes for the next five rounds. If the team fails to make a selection within the allotted time, the next team in order can move ahead of them. The "tardy" team can still make a selection at any time.

In 2011, the Baltimore Ravens lost their place while trying to negotiate a trade with the Chicago Bears. The Kansas City Chiefs moved ahead of Baltimore as the Ravens failed to complete the deal with Chicago.

The need for defined roles in the draft is crucial, and not all teams operated like the Bengals, who got everyone involved. But with the Bengals, the coach's opinion superseded the scout's. With some teams, the general manager has the final say.

And with a select few, the owner decides.

"Marvin Lewis would give us a handout of what he was looking for in each position, whether it was height, weight, or speed," Lippincott said. "Coaches have to be involved. Scouts are looking for production, coaches are looking for execution."

2

RINGING THE BELL

It was a special mission. Bert Bell, owner of the Philadelphia Eagles, had arrived at the University of Minnesota in 1933. He was there to negotiate a contract with the Gophers' star fullback and linebacker Stanley "King Kong" Kostka.

That's how it was done in those days: owners of NFL teams would stream to college campuses to sign contracts with the top players.

In this case Bell lost out on Kostka, who wound up with the NFL's Brooklyn Dodgers.

Bell's bitter disappointment couldn't be measured and set him off on another mission. "I made up my mind that this league would never survive unless we had some system whereby each team had an even chance to bid for talent against each other," Bell told the Associated Press.

At the time the NFL was dominated by a handful of teams that were competitive and made most of the money: the New York Giants, Chicago Bears, Washington Redskins, and Green Bay Packers. Teams such as Bell's Eagles were struggling financially. Hopeful of filling the empty seats at one point, Bell reduced ticket prices to one cent for kids.

At a league meeting in the 1930s, Bell put his proposal before the other owners: why not have a players' draft to create parity in the NFL? Teams could draft players in reverse order of their finish in the standings, thus giving the lower-end teams a chance to pick up some of the country's top college players.

At first some of the owners objected, particularly the Bears and Giants. But Bell eventually swung things his way.

And on February 8 and February 9, 1936, the NFL held its first draft. It took place at the Ritz Carlton in Philadelphia. That was a perfect place for the draft. The hotel happened to be owned by Bell's family.

"Franchise owners crowded into Bert Bell's hotel room, shucked their jackets, and cleared beds and bureaus for seating room," wrote the *New York Times*. "Bottles circulated, solemn oaths of league solidarity were taken, and the college stars were distributed."

Thus began an institution that, according to some of the sport's leading figures, saved professional football. At one point, legendary Bears owner George Halas called the college draft "the backbone of the sport." Halas made the remark while testifying in an antitrust hearing in Washington, D.C., in 1976.

Did the draft save pro football? You could actually make a case that Bell saved the game.

If he had done nothing else, insisted Hall of Fame sportswriter Arthur Daley of the *New York Times*, it would have been enough to qualify him for the Hall.

But there were other things, too, plenty of them.

Who was Bert Bell?

Born into a wealthy Philadelphia family, Bell eventually became an NFL commissioner who introduced a sweeping series of groundbreaking changes in the league that changed the game of football forever.

The NFL draft was just the first step for Bell in a colorful career cut short by a fatal heart attack in 1959, ironically while watching his beloved Eagles play.

Bell was one of pro football's most popular owners, a great host whenever owners got together for their meetings. His generosity was legendary, and the media loved him for his honesty and transparency.

At home, the conversation with Bert Bell, his wife, and three children was eclectic. Stop in at the Bell household, and you'd likely run into high-profile political figures or famous stars from the entertainment world.

Bell's family was connected politically. His maternal grandfather, Leonard Meyers, was a Civil War veteran and a member of Congress. A prominent Philadelphia attorney, Meyers was a close friend of Presidents Abraham Lincoln and James A. Garfield. He had an important voice in support of the so-called "Seward's Folly," William Seward's controversial purchase of Alaska from Russia in 1867.

Bert's brother, John C. Jr., was a nationally ranked tennis player and also a star in politics, serving as Pennsylvania's lieutenant governor and then governor for a short period. Later, he served a long term on the Pennsylvania Supreme Court.

So you can see there was more than a little political, and sports, talk around the dinner table.

"We were almost like the Kennedys in some ways," noted Upton Bell, Bert's son. "We would talk about everything, politics, sports, music, art, so it wasn't all sports, but we knew what was happening because when he got a call he didn't go in the other room, we just continued dinner."

One of the most fascinating figures at the table had to be Upton's mother, Frances Upton, at one time voted "the most beautiful woman in America." No kidding.

She was a showgirl who worked on the Broadway stage as a star in the Ziegfeld Follies. She played alongside such famed headliners as Eddie Cantor, Fanny Brice, and Ruth Etting, according to Upton, and helped introduce Cantor's iconic song, "Making Whoopie."

Frances Upton knew Al Capone and also "Machine Gun" Jack McGurn, two of the most famed (and dangerous) gangsters in the country.

"She knew everybody because in those days, most of the big shows were backed by gangsters," Upton said.

The Uptons were from Ireland and were always in touch with politics.

Frances Upton's grandfather, William Cleary Upton, wrote a controversial novel, *Uncle Pat's Cabin*, about life under English rule.

"It's still in libraries around America," Upton Bell said. "When he wrote the book, the British drove him out of Ireland."

William Cleary Upton came to New York and became chief of detectives in New York City. He spoke seven languages even though he never finished high school.

Born into one of Philadelphia's wealthiest families, Bell was christened de Benneville. Preferring just plain Bert, he made an early name for himself as captain of the Penn football team.

"He threw the first pass in Rose Bowl history," Upton said. "That's when the Ivy League was among the powers of the country."

That was 1917, and America was getting involved in World War I.

In his junior year, Bell volunteered to fight in the war. He was decorated by General John J. Pershing for valor in the field, according to Upton Bell.

Following the war, Bell came back and finished his final year as captain and quarterback for the University of Pennsylvania. For a while, Bell had a hard time getting his life in order.

"In those days it was party time," Upton Bell said. "It was part of Philadelphia society. They went to all the parties in Saratoga and all over the country. They all knew each other."

Born to wealth, Bert Bell lost most of his personal fortune with his free-spending ways. Things quieted down when he met Frances Upton and asked her to marry him.

But first he had to change his lifestyle. He had to be more conservative if he wanted to marry her. Frances was a devout Catholic and wouldn't marry anyone who was drinking.

"Father stopped drinking alcohol to marry mother," Upton said. "He said, 'I won't take a drink for the rest of my life.' He never did."

On the very day of their wedding, Bert Bell had a major request for his bride to be. Short of cash, he talked her into a loan to buy the Frankford Yellow Jackets out of bankruptcy.

She obliged, and they gave themselves a football team as a wedding present. The franchise wasn't called the Eagles yet—not until Bert Bell walked by a sign showing the eagle on the National Recovery Act, and he said, "That's it! That's what I will name it."

As the family sat down for dinner, a telephone was strategically placed on the table so Bell could reach it easily.

"The telephone was on the table and when calls would come in, he never turned down a phone call," Upton Bell said. "We could hear his conversations at dinner about what was going on in the league."

Quietly or noisily, Bell started to shape pro football during his administration.

"He was first to say, 'I am going to schedule the weak against the weak and the strong against the strong so by the middle of the season, everybody is still in the race,'" Upton Bell said. "He made up the schedule himself. That helped the game. When asked by a writer, he said, 'I am very happy today, because on any given Sunday, any team can beat any other team.'"

Any given Sunday. The phrase became the code word around the NFL.

"It happened quickly," Bell said. "The Colts in the 1958 championship game were built through the waiver wire and the draft. Most of the guys that were there, including Johnny Unitas, were free agents. They went from nothing to that."

The waiver wire, another Bell institution. "The lower teams had first dibs on anyone that was put on waivers."

Bell was equally trusted by the media, the players, and the owners. He pushed through the first player association and started a pension for the players. He told the owners, if they wouldn't recognize it, they would have to fire him. They didn't.

As commissioner, Bell showed a sense of fair play rarely seen in commissioners of sports leagues. Bell is one of those rarities, a person who played the game, owned a team, and served as the sport's commissioner.

His relationship with reporters was second to none. "He never hid anything from the press," Upton said. "No BS."

A dozen years after the introduction of the draft, after the NFL had struck gold with the sudden-death 1958 championship game between the New York Giants and the Baltimore Colts, Bell was still working hard to develop the professional game.

At first Bell proposed Saturday-night football. But when the colleges objected because they thought it would hurt their game, Bell backed off. Televised games at night eventually became standard fare for the league. See Monday-night football.

"After the league had finally made it in 1959," said Upton Bell, "my father said he still worried about the poor teams."

He needn't have worried too much. The draft was helping every other team catch up.

"My father was always in favor of poor teams having a chance to catch up quickly," Upton Bell said. "And as you know, after three years of good drafts, even then, and you're right back in it."

"Look at the Steelers [in the 1970s]. Chuck Noll and I worked together in Baltimore, and when Noll went [to Pittsburgh], after the first really bad year, look at those four, five drafts that propelled the Steelers and Dolphins in the '70s and all of their players were acquired through the draft."

Along with the NFL draft, here are some of Bell's other accomplishments and innovations as NFL commissioner from 1946 to 1959:

- One year after taking office, he proposed sudden death in championship games to avoid the risk of cochampions.
- He introduced a television policy that included local blackouts so teams wouldn't be competing against themselves. Bell was responsible for the first seven-figure TV contract.
- He negotiated the NFL's merger with the upstart All-America Football Conference in 1949.

Bell was particularly alert to gambling issues, particularly any bribe attempts by gamblers to fix the outcome of games. Attempts to fix games have been going on in sports for as long as anyone could remember.

Commissioner Kenesaw Mountain Landis, for one, had his problems in baseball with the Black Sox scandal when Chicago White Sox players received bribe money to throw the 1919 World Series.

The very first year Bell took office, he was faced with his own scandal when two players with the Giants were approached by gamblers to fix a game. Not just any game, but the 1946 championship contest between the New York Giants and Chicago Bears.

Sidney Paris, a convicted felon who had served four years for mail fraud, had met Giants fullback Merle Hapes at an Elks Lodge meeting in November 1946. Hapes introduced Paris to Giants quarterback Frank Filchock. Eventually, after a series of social gatherings, the gambler offered the two players $2,500 each to make sure that the Bears won the championship game by at least 10 points. According to one report, Paris said he would also put down a $1,000 bet for each of them. The players were reportedly offered off-season jobs as well that would net them another $15,000 apiece.

Filchock, a Pittsburgh Pirates (now Steelers) second-round draft choice in 1938, had arrived in New York via a trade. He had played with the Washington Redskins, alternating with the great Sammy Baugh, before becoming a star in New York.

Hapes, a bruising fullback from the University of Mississippi, was the Giants' first-round draft pick in 1942. He played for the Giants in 1942 and 1946 in a career interrupted by the Second World War.

Baseball and football weren't the only sports affected by gamblers in this time. Gamblers who had fixed college basketball games were being investigated and some already sent to prison. While tapping the gamblers' phones for more basketball cheaters, law enforcement authorities came up with the names of Filchock and Hapes.

That triggered a lightning response from authorities. The day before the game, Bell, Giants owner Tim Mara, and police commissioner Arthur Wallander had met in the office of New York City mayor Bill O'Dwyer to assess the situation. O'Dwyer also wanted to meet the players. Later that day, Filchock and Hapes were brought into the mayor's residence.

In his chat with the mayor, Filchock denied being approached by gamblers. Hapes admitted he was approached but failed to report the bribe attempt. To some, this was a greater sin.

Since neither player had taken any bribes, authorities concluded that the matter should be left in Bell's hands. What was the commissioner to do?

Bell's conclusions: Never mind that Hapes did not take a bribe; he was guilty of conversing with a known gambler as far as Bell was concerned. The commissioner barred the fullback right before the championship game.

Because Filchock admitted he did not talk to the gamblers, he was allowed to play. And play, he did.

When his name was introduced over the loudspeaker system, Filchock was roundly booed by the fans. Despite suffering a broken nose, Filchock played 50 minutes and accounted for all of the Giants' scoring. His numbers at the end of a 24–14 loss to the Bears were 9 of 26 passes for two touchdowns, and 128 yards and six interceptions.

It was Filchock's last hurrah in the NFL, as well as Hapes's. The two were subsequently indefinitely suspended from playing professional football in the United States and spent the rest of their careers competing in Canada. Bell laid down the law, he said, because the players "were guilty of actions detrimental to the welfare of the National Football League and of professional football."

So it was as well with another scandal that shook up the NFL 17 years later when Paul Hornung and Alex Karras were suspended by commissioner Pete Rozelle for gambling. Hornung, the Green Bay Packers' star running back, and Karras, the All-Pro defensive lineman for the Detroit Lions, missed out on the entire 1963 season when they were at the top of their game.

Both players were so contrite that Rozelle reopened the doors for them in 1964. They came back to continue their careers, and Hornung, the Notre Dame running back who was the overall No. 1 pick at the 1957 draft by Green Bay, eventually found his way into the Hall of Fame after an overly long wait.

Karras had been the first-round pick of the Detroit Lions in 1958 after starring at Iowa.

Another notable scandal two decades later involved compulsive gambler Art Schlichter, who served a jail term for various illegal activities.

Schlichter, the Ohio State quarterback, had been a first-round pick at the 1982 draft by the Baltimore Colts.

By this time, thanks to Bell, football owners had been keeping close tabs on their teams to make sure there would not be even a hint of impropriety. Following the 1946 championship game, Bell had closely monitored swings in football betting lines. He tightened up security by bringing in retired FBI agents as security officers throughout the NFL.

The next year he took on the All-America Football Conference (AAFC), a new league that hoped to challenge the NFL. Some of the NFL owners had recommended that Bell crush the competition. Instead, Bell sat down with the upstart league and worked out a merger that allowed the AAFC's three strongest teams to join the NFL—the San Francisco 49ers, the Baltimore Colts, and the Cleveland Browns.

Bell's ace in the hole to clinch the deal: his extreme popularity.

"He was equally trusted by the media, the players, and the owners," Upton Bell said. "You would never get that again. I don't know any commissioner today that is trusted by everyone. When was the last commissioner that actually played the game? Any sport. Did anyone play the game, own a team, and become commissioner? Bert Bell understood it from every level. That's what separates him from everyone, including the commissioners of today."

3

THE FIRST

The telegram arrived at Jay Berwanger's fraternity house at the University of Chicago in 1935.

"It really had no significance for me," Berwanger said. "I got a wire at my frat house and tickets to go to New York. I looked forward more to that than to the award."

That's how the first Heisman Trophy winner was notified of his prize. It wasn't called the Heisman then, just the "Downtown Athletic Club Trophy," handed out to the top college football player in the country.

Berwanger would later add another first to his résumé when he was selected as the No. 1 overall pick of the initial NFL draft in 1936, by the Philadelphia Eagles. That's as far as his football career would go.

"I really wasn't interested in pro ball," said Berwanger. "They weren't paying any money, something like $100 a game. You couldn't blame them. This was following the Depression, and nobody had any money."

Not even Chicago Bears owner George Halas could convince Berwanger to join the pros. A friend of Berwanger's, Halas obtained the rights to the star player from the Eagles. He didn't get much more than the rights.

"We didn't have any real serious talks," said Berwanger, a two-time All-American. "I told him $25,000 for two years, no cut. I was being slightly facetious. He said, 'Good night, it was nice talking to you. Have a good time.' There was no bitterness."

Turning down a football contract wasn't all that uncommon in those days, when the pros ranked a distant second to the college game in the American sports scene. The next two Heisman Trophy winners, Larry Kelly and Clint Frank, both stars at Yale, did not play pro football. Quarterback Davey O'Brien of Texas Christian University (TCU) was the first Heisman winner to sign a pro contract. Picked No. 4 overall in the 1939 draft, he received a $12,000 bonus from the Eagles for a two-year contract. O'Brien only played two years in the NFL before leaving pro football for a career with the FBI.

By comparison, the NFL draft in the 1930s produced a number of players who would reach immortality after long and thrilling careers. Among them were Sammy Baugh, Sid Luckman, and Clarence "Ace" Parker, all ticketed for the Hall of Fame. All three became trailblazers as the NFL moved forward to a new age of football emphasizing the forward pass.

Baugh, a quarterback out of TCU, was the No. 6 pick by the Washington Redskins in the 1937 draft. Parker, an All-American tailback/halfback from Duke, was selected by the Brooklyn Dodgers football franchise with the third pick in the second round in 1937. Luckman, an All-American quarterback at Columbia, was picked by the Chicago Bears, second overall in 1939.

They would all be part of an era of dramatic change in the NFL spawned by Bert Bell, the former Eagles owner and an NFL commissioner from 1946 to 1959. Under Bell, the NFL draft was born, a plan that made copycats out of other professional sports leagues in America.

In a time when the University of Chicago played in the Big Ten, the six-foot, 195-pound Berwanger literally did it all for his team. He was listed as a tailback in a single-wing offense but also passed the ball, punted, kicked off, and kicked extra points. On defense, Berwanger played linebacker for the first three downs and then usually dropped back to receive punts. Once in a game against Minnesota, he made an incredible 14 tackles in the first half.

Born March 19, 1914, in Dubuque, Iowa, Berwanger starred in high school there before playing at the University of Chicago.

Playing on both sides of the ball for a mediocre team from 1933 to 1935, Berwanger rushed for 1,839 yards and scored 22 touchdowns in 23 college games. He was an All-American in 1934 and 1935 and team captain as well as president of his senior class.

The rugged Berwanger missed only one game in his entire college career and that because of a knee injury. He shrugged off other injuries such as a broken nose. He had also broken his nose in high school and told the *New York Times*, "I was told if I broke it again, I wouldn't have any nose to repair."

The fearless Berwanger merely slapped on a face mask and went out to play. He was believed to be one of the first players in the early days of football to wear a face mask attached to his helmet.

Ohio State coach Francis Schmidt called Berwanger the best back his team had faced since the great Red Grange. According to the *New York Times*, a friend noted that teams had suicide squads that went after Berwanger. To get him out of the game meant a "cinch win."

President Gerald Ford, who played football at Michigan, once recalled a meeting with the rugged Berwanger and his Chicago team.

"When I tackled Jay," Ford remembered for the *New York Times*, "his heel hit my cheek bone and opened it up three inches."

Said Berwanger, "When we met again, he turned his cheek and showed me a scar on the side of his face. He told me, 'I got this trying to tackle you in the Chicago-Michigan game.'"

When the telegram from the Downtown Athletic Club invited Berwanger to New York, he recalled, "There was no anticipation as there is today."

He does remember that a fuss was made over him. "They had a great affair, and I was treated royally. I stayed at the Downtown Athletic Club, and out of my window I could see the Statue of Liberty. That was thrilling."

Other thrills: seeing the high-kicking Rockette showgirls at Radio City Music Hall and lunch at another New York landmark, the famed 21 Club.

For a while, Berwanger found work as a newspaper columnist, a coach at the University of Chicago, and a speechmaker. "I made speeches for $100 to $150, so it came out all right financially for me."

Berwanger eventually became a successful rubber and plastics manufacturer following a stint as a navy flight instructor during World War II. He kept in touch with football as an intramural coach at Chicago and as a Big Ten game official.

Berwanger said the Downtown Athletic Club award didn't open many doors for him in the business world, but "it made a good conversation piece."

THREE FOR THE AGES

Sid Luckman

Like Berwanger, Luckman was a player much coveted by the Bears' Halas. And like Berwanger, Luckman was reticent to turn pro. That is, until Halas visited him twice in New York and offered him a $5,000 contract that was the highest in pro football at the time.

Halas had traded two players and a draft choice to the Pittsburgh Steelers for their first-round choice. It turned out to be the steal of the century.

"When I was reading the paper that I had been drafted by the Bears, it was certainly a tremendous surprise," said the five-foot-eleven, 190-pound Luckman. "But I had a very nice job and that's where I thought my future was going to be."

That quickly changed with the contract offering.

"When he gave me the contract, and I signed it, he said, 'You and Jesus Christ are the only two I would pay $5,000.' I said, 'Coach, you put me in some pretty good company.'"

Luckman, a native of Brooklyn, New York, had never been farther than Buffalo. He thought Chicago was where cowboys were still riding the range toting six-guns.

What did Luckman have that was worth so much money and so many players to the Bears?

Halas had scouted Luckman when he played at Columbia under the famed Lou Little. The Bears' owner-coach had invented a new type of offensive setup called the "T-Formation."

It was used by the offense in which three running backs lined up in a row about five yards behind the quarterback forming the shape of a *T*. There have been many variations since.

Halas believed that the strong-armed Luckman was the right quarterback to execute such a formation. Luckman wasn't so sure after the third day of practice in the Bears' camp. He thought he was too small to play in the pros.

"The linemen came in, and I knew then this was going to be a struggle, walking into that dressing room and seeing these 'Monsters of the Midway,' they were so big and fast," Luckman said in an interview with the *Chicago Tribune* in 1995. "All my high school and college career, I had never seen anything like these athletes."

Luckman played his high school ball in Brooklyn before attending Columbia, where he was an All-American in 1938. He gained national repute when he made the cover of *Life* magazine with the headline "Best Passer."

If not for a savior in Little, Luckman possibly wouldn't have graduated from college. In his freshman year, Luckman was having financial problems—there were no athletic scholarships at the Ivy League school—when Little stepped in and found a number of jobs for his quarterback.

Luckman, whose father died when he was a young boy, found another father figure in Halas.

"George Halas told us that football was a means to an end," Luckman told the Associated Press. "All of us had to seek a way to keep up our income, because you never really know what could happen on any given Sunday."

As fate would have it, Luckman's first game in the pros was against his hometown New York Giants. The Bears lost 16–14, but that wasn't the most memorable part for Luckman.

"You'll never know the emotion, the stress," Luckman said of that game. "That had to be the most emotional time in my football history. My family, my friends from college, the Columbia coaches, the dean of the college . . . they were all at the game."

Luckman preferred to remember another performance against Washington the following season when the Bears whacked the Redskins by a record 73–0 to win the NFL title. The losing quarterback in the title game was none other than Baugh, who would eventually join Luckman in the Pro Football Hall of Fame.

After 12 seasons with the Bears, Luckman retired as team leader in touchdowns (137) and yards gained (14,686). Luckman was voted the NFL's top player three times and selected an All-Pro five times while leading the Bears to four league championships.

He left an indelible mark on football, summed up in part by the three sentences he wanted written on his gravestone: "He had it all. He did it all. He loved it all."

Sammy Baugh

The same can be said of Baugh, a remarkable all-around athlete who did just about everything for the Redskins. With his phenomenal passing skills, Baugh played a role in pioneering the use of the forward pass in both college and the pros.

Before Baugh appeared on the scene, professional football was almost totally reliant on a bruising three-yards-and-a-cloud-of-dust ground game. It was unusual for a quarterback, or a tailback in most cases, to throw the ball more than a few times in a game. With Washington, Baugh threw passes from the single-wing tailback position before mastering the position of a T-formation quarterback.

Baugh once thought about making baseball a career instead of football. He earned the nickname "Slingin' Sammy" as a young baseball player with a powerful arm. He tried out as a shortstop with the St. Louis Cardinals. But after a session in the Cardinals' training camp, he decided to stick to football.

It was the appropriate choice, considering what happened over the next 16 seasons. From 1937 to 1952, Baugh helped revolutionize the game with his prowess as a two-way player. He was a combination quarterback-punter-defensive back whose records on both sides of the ball will stand forever due to the evolution of the game.

Take note of Baugh's remarkable 1943 season when he led the NFL in passing, intercepted 11 passes by his opponents, and led the league with a punting average of 45.9 yards.

Born in Temple, Texas, in 1914, Baugh moved with his family to Sweetwater. As a youngster he worked on his passing skills by hanging a tire on a rope in his backyard and throwing the ball through it. At TCU, he became a two-time All-American.

Baugh led TCU to the national championship and then was a force from the start of his pro career. As a rookie playing in the NFL's championship game, Baugh threw for three touchdowns on frozen turf at Wrigley Field in Chicago to lift the Redskins to a 28–21 victory over the Bears in the title game.

The Redskins and Bears would meet again for the title in 1940, this time with a far different result when the Bears swamped Washington 73–0 in the NFL's most lopsided score. Baugh shrugged off that monumental loss by leading the Redskins to another NFL championship in 1942—again over the Bears.

The game once more featured the two preeminent passers of their day in Baugh and Luckman. It was inevitable there would be continual comparisons made between the pair with each at the zenith of his career.

Eddie LeBaron, who took over as Washington's quarterback after Baugh retired, called him "tremendously accurate."

"He could always find a way to throw it off-balance," LeBaron told *Newsday* in a 2002 interview. "I've seen him throw the ball overarm, sidearm, and underarm and complete them."

In his first season in the NFL, Baugh completed a record 81 passes—about seven a game—for 1,127 yards. In comparison, there were only six passers who averaged as much as three completions that year.

The story is told in the *New York Times* of Baugh's first practice session with the Redskins when his coach, Ray Flaherty, handed Baugh a football.

"They tell me you're quite a passer," the coach remarked.

"I reckon I can throw a little," Baugh responded.

"Show me," Flaherty said. "Hit that receiver in the eye."

To which Baugh supposedly replied, "Which eye?"

In physical stature, Baugh was one of the tallest players in the league at six foot three, 180 pounds, the better to find his receivers streaming downfield. He was a combination of finesse and toughness. He once told this story on himself to the *San Antonio Express-News*: "One time there was a defensive lineman who was coming down on me with his fists closed. A couple of plays later, I found a play we could waste and I told our linemen to just let him come through. The guy got about five feet from me, and I hit him right in the forehead with the ball. He turned red and passed out. It scared the hell out of me."

Though a tall, inviting target for opposing defenses, Baugh managed to stay injury free through his 16 years of service in the NFL. "The only time I got hurt was when I got a broken rib from a young steer's horn," Baugh told the *Chicago Tribune*.

Following his NFL career, Baugh remained in football coaching at both the college and professional level. He became the first coach of the American Football League's (AFL) New York Titans, who were then years away from the merger with the NFL. He coached in New York for two years.

"Sammy was a great innovator, but he kept it all in his head," recalled star linebacker Larry Grantham, who was drafted by both the Baltimore Colts and the Titans. "Our playbook was like a thin composition book, but he really knew a lot of football. He just didn't put it down (on paper). Sammy was a great innovator as far as offensive football. He would watch other teams line up and he knew exactly what plays would work against a defense. Our success, whatever we had, was because of Sammy's brilliance on offense."

Baugh was among the NFL's inaugural Hall of Fame class of 1963 and later was chosen as one of four quarterbacks on the league's 75th-anniversary team.

Ace Parker

Clarence "Ace" Parker was one of the last great tailback stars in the single wing, a run-oriented formation that for many years was the bread and butter of the NFL. The shifty Parker did more than just run in the ancient era of two-way football that featured leather helmets with no face masks and high-top shoes. He caught passes, punted, placekicked, and was also a star in the defensive backfield.

Parker was a second-round pick in the NFL draft, 13th overall, by the old Brooklyn Dodgers. He didn't waste any time establishing himself as one of the top players in the league. Despite playing part of the 1940 season wearing a 10-pound brace after injuring his ankle, Parker was voted the NFL's top player that season.

From 1938 to 1940, Parker was an All-Pro in an era when the NFL produced the likes of Baugh, Luckman, and Don Hutson, all future Hall of Famers.

Parker was born in Portsmouth, Virginia, in 1912. A five-sport letterman at Portsmouth's Wilson High School, he displayed his supreme golfing talents when he beat Hall of Fame golfer and fellow Virginian Sam Snead in a long driving contest.

At Duke, Parker played both football and baseball. He had first envisioned a major league career for himself. He signed to play for Connie Mack's Philadelphia Athletics and actually hit a home run in his first at-bat. It was one of the few highlights in his two years in pro baseball, which was quickly put behind him for good. A brilliant all-around athlete, Parker would find his greatest glories on the gridiron.

Parker's nickname was dreamed up by a sportswriter at Duke when he pronounced Parker his team's "ace in the hole."

Listed at five foot ten and 178 pounds, a typical size for a back of his day, Parker very often took over a game by himself.

One example came in the Dodgers' victory over the Cleveland Rams in 1940, when Parker was involved in all of his team's 29 points. He passed for two touchdowns (TDs), scored another after an interception, set up one more TD with another interception, and kicked two extra points. He wasn't too busy either to serve as holder for a field goal.

World War II interrupted Parker's football career before he returned to play for the Boston Yanks in 1945. He finished the following season with the New York Yankees of the rival All-America Football Conference.

Parker continued to play and manage baseball in the minor leagues. He then returned to Duke to work as an assistant football coach and head baseball coach from 1953 to 1966. Among the football players coached by Parker was Hall of Famer Sonny Jurgensen. Parker later worked as a scout for NFL teams before retiring.

4

AFRICAN AMERICAN
BREAKTHROUGH

For Kenny Washington, it was a matter of timing, too early to make history. For Wally Triplett, making history was something that just came naturally.

Each football player was a product of a different era but faced a common enemy: racism.

"When I came to the NFL, it was a very prejudiced league," said Triplett, a tailback who was the first black selected in the NFL draft to take the field in a league game.

That was the 1950s, still not exactly an age of enlightenment in the NFL but slowly starting to make a turn in the right direction.

Not so in the time of Washington, who despite his great talent as a running back with the University of California, Los Angeles (UCLA) football team was shut out of NFL participation for a major portion of his professional career. Despite his reputation as one of the country's great and most popular college players, not one NFL team drafted Washington, who had finished sixth in the Heisman Trophy balloting in 1939.

The story is told about Chicago Bears owner George Halas, who expressed interest in Washington. Following the college all-star game in Soldier Field in which Washington had distinguished himself with a touchdown, Halas approached Washington and told him to sit tight. Don't return to Los Angeles, he was told. The Bears were thinking of signing him.

One week later, Washington still hadn't heard from Halas. Washington headed back to California to engage in minor league football along with Woody Strode. Washington and Strode played, and starred for, the Hollywood Bears of the Pacific Coast Football League (PCFL).

Washington wasn't completely finished with the National Football League. His knees damaged by playing in the PCFL, clearly he had left his better days behind when he signed with the Los Angeles Rams on March 21, 1946.

Washington's signing was a concession to placate the Los Angeles Coliseum Commission and make it easier for the Rams to get a lease. The Rams later signed Strode, a black end who also had seen better days on the gridiron.

Strode and Washington met in 1936 as freshmen at UCLA, a completely liberal school when it came to sports figures. A Los Angeles sportswriter had termed Washington and Strode "The Goal Dust Twins," a play of words on Fairbanks's Gold Dust, a popular soap powder.

"The Coliseum people warned the Rams if they practiced discrimination, they couldn't use the stadium," Washington said later. "When those NFL people began thinking about all those seats and the money they could make filling them up, they decided my kind wasn't so bad after all."

Like Triplett, Washington was a trailblazer.

Before the first NFL draft in 1936, there had been a smattering of black players in pro football, starting with Charles Follis in 1904. Follis was paid to play for the Shelby (Ohio) Athletic Club.

In 1920, Fritz Pollard was the first great black star, playing for the Akron Pros in a league that was the forerunner of the NFL.

According to the Pro Football Researchers Association (PFRA), 13 black players appeared in the NFL between the league's first season (1920) and 1933. The NFL was an all-white league from 1934 until Washington signed with the Rams 12 years later. The numbers grew slowly. In 1950, blacks in the NFL totaled 14 players.

In making his breakthrough in 1946, Washington was a year ahead of Jackie Robinson, his UCLA football teammate who would create his own history in 1947 in breaking the color line in baseball's major leagues.

Before he made his major league debut with the Brooklyn Dodgers, Robinson played in the same backfield with Washington. Writing for *Gridiron* magazine in 1971, Robinson called Washington "the greatest football player I have ever seen." Robinson also said he was sure Washington had a "deep hurt" that he never became a national figure in professional sports.

One of many typical college performances for Washington came against crosstown rival Southern Cal in 1937.

Trailing the Trojans 19–0 with five minutes left, Washington passed for two touchdowns in 29 seconds. He later had a great opportunity to win the game when he threw a pass to Strode at the one-yard line. But Strode dropped the ball in the final seconds, allowing the Trojans to steal one.

Even in losing, Washington had put on a remarkable display from his tailback position.

Watching Washington's late-game magic, Southern Cal coach Howard Jones was a nervous wreck by the end of the game. UCLA coach Bill Spaulding went to the University of Southern California (USC) locker room to offer congratulations to Jones. The door to Jones's office was closed.

Spaulding knocked and someone inside the office asked who was there.

"Bill Spaulding," the UCLA coach said. "Tell Howard he can come out now. We've stopped passing."

Washington's most glorious time was the 1930s and early 1940s.

Washington was a star halfback at Los Angeles Lincoln High School before joining UCLA. Assessing Washington's performance in the 1937 college season, the *Illustrated Football Annual* stated, "Washington is by far the most accurate passer west of the Rockies."

Washington, a fleet six-foot-one, 195-pound specimen, was a halfback who was a model of versatility, whether passing, punting, blocking, pass defending, or ball carrying—both inside and outside.

He scored 19 career touchdowns and set five Bruins records, including career total offense (3,206 yards). Playing against the feared Washington, opposing teams in the Pacific Coast Conference (later named the Pac-8 and now the Pac-12) usually voted him the greatest player they faced all season, whether winning or losing the game.

In 1939, a national magazine dubbed Washington "Back of the Year" after he led the nation in total yards as a senior and played 580 of a possible 600 minutes. He was voted to the All-America team.

Washington grew up in Lincoln Heights, California, raised mostly by his grandmother and an uncle, who would become the first black uniformed lieutenant in the Los Angeles Police Department.

The pigeon-toed Washington ran with extraordinary power, usually using a powerful straight-arm to bully opponents.

"He had a crazy gait, like he had two broken legs," teammate Tom Harmon told *Sports Illustrated* in a 1990 interview. "He'd be coming at you straight, and it would look like he was going sideways."

As the first African American to be drafted by an NFL team and actually play in a league game, Wally Triplett became an historic figure. It was just another milestone for Triplett.

When Triplett was drafted by the Lions in 1949 out of Penn State, the NFL was engaged in a war for players with the All-America Football Conference (AAFC).

"[The NFL] was a very prejudiced, old, rough league," Triplett recalled. "And here comes this upstart league which sought out a lot of the big kids from schools and started to compete with the NFL. So the NFL held mostly to their policy of discrimination, and they did not seek to draft anybody until I came along. And they relented and drafted me."

At the same time, Triplett was being courted by the AAFC's Brooklyn Dodgers. Triplett said that Dodgers general manager Branch Rickey, who was instrumental in bringing Robinson to baseball's big leagues, was "cheap."

"After discussing terms with him, I said I'll go ahead with Detroit," Triplett said. "They were offering me a few more dollars. It was about a $700 difference."

Triplett didn't wait long before making an impact on his new team.

In his first year in the NFL, Triplett set a Lions record with an 80-yard touchdown run from scrimmage against the Packers. Then on October 29, 1950, Triplett had an even more spectacular day, the game of his life, against the Los Angeles Rams.

The five-foot-ten, 173-pound Triplett returned four kickoffs for a total of 294 yards. Highlighted was a 97-yard return for a touchdown, one of three he scored that day. The record stood for 44 years.

"I thought this was the easiest thing going," Triplett said.

Triplett's debut with the Lions was just another leap into uncharted territory for him, both on and off the football field. Triplett had established a legacy at Penn State as the first African American to start for the Nittany Lions football team. Along with Dennie Hoggard, Triplett later starred on the great 1947 Penn

State team that went to the Cotton Bowl, another first for black players.

Not that life was easy as an athlete at "Happy" Valley. Despite a reputation as a liberal school, Penn State had some segregationist policies in place when Triplett walked through the university's doors in 1946.

Before Triplett made the team, he was told by coach Bob Higgins that he had to room in Lincoln Hall, "where the colored athletes live." One of his roommates was Barney Ewell, the track and field great.

Triplett hailed from La Mott, Pennsylvania, a small upscale community just north of Philadelphia. A three-sport star at Cheltenham High School, Triplett attended Penn State on a senatorial scholarship that had nothing to do with football.

At first his relationship with Higgins wasn't very smooth.

"He and I didn't hit it off because he thought I was a rich intellectual kid from suburban Philadelphia," Triplett said. "He was used to—and wanted—all those poor, rough boys from western Pennsylvania."

Triplett was an independent sort. "I guess I was cocky," he said. "I was able to take care of myself."

On the way to his first meeting with Higgins, Triplett spotted a sign in a bus station advertising for a dishwasher. Triplett took the job so he could have some extra spending money.

"The Penn State athletic department was always worried about where they were going to find players work and where players could eat," Triplett said. "Most of the guys worked in the fraternity houses. They would get their meals and pin money. So I had a job, and I could get my meals."

In 1946, Penn State was scheduled to face Miami, a segregated school that would not allow its athletes to play with black athletes. It was common then for many colleges to leave their black athletes at home when they played the Hurricanes and other schools in the South.

As game time approached, Triplett and Hoggard weren't sure they would be making the trip. Finally, a meeting was set up by the players to discuss the controversial issue. The players decided to cancel the game, establishing a precedent. The Nittany Lions simply refused to play in a game where the whole team wasn't welcome.

"We are Penn State!" It was the unifying cry that would become a tradition at Happy Valley. Supposedly it was born at one of these team meetings emphasizing the team's stand on the racial issue: we stand together as a team.

"When the team took the stand they did, I was very surprised," Triplett said. "I have always been quite proud of those guys. It became a part of the history of Penn State football and vaulted the school into the limelight."

Higgins began to appreciate Triplett as the 1947 season progressed, and the Nittany Lions had a special season. The '47 team put together one of the finest defensive efforts in college football history. With Triplett playing on both sides of the ball, Penn State established all kinds of records.

"We got mad if somebody made two, three yards," Triplett said. "That used to be our cry: 'Give 'em nothing.'"

In one game, the Nittany Lions gave them less than nothing. They established the National Collegiate Athletic Association (NCAA) mark for the fewest yards allowed in a game—minus 47 against Syracuse—on their way to a 9–0 season.

That earned the Lions a No. 4 ranking in the country and a bid to the Cotton Bowl in Dallas, Texas. Their opponent: Southern Methodist University (SMU). That is, if SMU, a segregated school in a segregated city, agreed to play against the Lions' two black players.

When word came down, "Southern Methodist said they would break their color barrier," Triplett recalled.

There was one consideration: housing.

"The manager of athletics at that time went down to Dallas in advance, like you normally do for any bowl game, to make all the arrangements," recalled Ed Czekaj, one of the Penn State players.

"When he got down there he found out that nobody would house the football team because we had two blacks on the squad. So we got hold of a couple alumni in the area, and they had a few contacts with the people at the navy base between Dallas and Fort Worth."

The navy people consented to house the team at the barracks.

"Thank God they did, or I don't know where we would have stayed," Czekaj said.

The base was located 18 miles north of Dallas. And it wasn't exactly the lap of luxury.

"We were all 26, 27, 28 years old, four or five years in the service, and we went down there for a bowl game and had to sleep in double-decker bunks. It was just like our World War II days . . . we even dined on navy chow."

As for entertainment, there was very little of it.

"We were locked up in the barracks, and they showed old movies that we had seen three or four times," Czekaj said.

The players became disgruntled, pleading with Higgins to get them off base for some entertainment.

"They took us to the top of a bank building. It was supposed to be the tallest building in Dallas. That was our big sightseeing trip for the week."

Practices were hindered by bad weather, the Lions tuning up for the biggest game of the year in rain, sleet, and snow. And to many, it was more than a game. "It was history-making, both socially and athletically," Triplett said.

The integration included fans as well as players. Hoggard's mother, the wife of a state senator, came to the game as part of the Pennsylvania delegation.

"They had her sitting on the 50-yard line with everybody else," Triplett said. "That was a big thing."

Triplett and Hoggard would thus be making history as the first African Americans to play in the Cotton Bowl game. As it would happen, Triplett played a big part in a brilliant contest.

The Nittany Lions trailed 13–0 before staging a late rally. With less than two minutes left in the first half, Penn State quarterback Elwood Petchel fired a 36-yard touchdown pass to cut SMU's lead to 13–7. Powered by the running of Fran Rogel and Petchel's passing, Penn State moved to SMU's four-yard line late in the third period. Then Petchel on the run threw a pass into the waiting arms of Triplett, who fittingly played 58 of the game's 60 minutes.

Final score: Penn State 13, SMU 13.

The game ended Triplett's career at Penn State. During his three seasons from 1946 to 1948, the Lions were a national powerhouse with a 22–3–2 record. The Lions lost the three games by a mere 17 points total.

In one of their biggest victories, the Lions stopped Navy and spoiled president Harry Truman's day. "He refused to come into the locker room," Triplett said.

As a senior, Triplett led the Lions in scoring with 36 points and all-purpose yardage (424 rushing, 90 receiving, and 220 punt returns).

Next stop: the NFL.

The Lions made Triplett the third African American selected in the draft. He became the first of the 1949 draftees to take the field in a league game. Other blacks had been picked up by NFL teams but not in the draft.

Playing in the NFL wasn't always comfortable for Triplett, or for the other blacks in the league. Triplett credited a newspaperman, Bill Matney of the *Michigan Chronicle*, for helping the black athletes. "He worked tirelessly trying to fight prejudice in the NFL," Triplett said.

Occasionally, problems would crop up, Triplett said.

One year "we were supposed to play the Redskins in Washington, but they would not let us come in the stadium. In a preseason game in New Orleans against the Eagles, we could not stay in the hotel, and they refused to let us in the stadium. In 1949, there were only five black players in the NFL. I was always conscious of the color aspect, as you had to be to survive since it was what was propelling so much of what was going on."

Black players from football and other Detroit sports teams hung out together off the field.

"We could not go to the same places as the white players," Triplett said, "so we used to go down to the Black Bottom after the game. The Detroit Stars (of baseball's Negro Leagues) and the basketball players who used to play at Brewster Center all bonded together, because we were all going through the same prejudiced thing." Black Bottom was a predominantly black neighborhood on Detroit's east side known for its significant contribution to American music. At one point, Brewster Center was the largest housing project owned by the city of Detroit.

Triplett's football career was cut short by the Korean War. He became one of the first NFL players drafted during that conflict. When he came home following military service, the Lions traded him to the Chicago Cardinals. He retired from pro football in 1953.

"Then I looked for a job."

Triplett found one in Detroit's racing industry. It was another breakthrough for him as he became the first black racing clerk in Detroit. "I stayed with it, and that was part of my résumé for 35 years," Triplett said.

A résumé deserving of the word pioneer.

UNWRITTEN LAW

Ron Mix, a longtime star in the American Football League in the 1960s, believes there might have been a quota system for blacks in the NFL in his days.

"There was a rumor that there was an unwritten law in the NFL: no more than five black players [per team]," Mix said. "I don't know if this was true or not, but there weren't that many black players in the NFL on each team.

"Look at the Washington Redskins. I don't think they had a black player until the middle sixties [actually 1962]. But clearly, the NFL was not making any effort to bring in black players."

Not so the rival AFL, which *aggressively* battled the NFL for players in the 1960s.

"They couldn't afford not to be color blind," Mix said. "They needed to bring in the best talent.

"The AFL brought in a lot of great black players. I wasn't part of the decision-making process, but I could only look at what the end result was. There were far more black players per team in the AFL than there was in the NFL."

5

THE WAR BETWEEN
THE LEAGUES

The Los Angeles Rams were thrilled when they signed Billy Cannon to a contract in 1960.

No sooner had Louisiana State's Heisman Trophy winner agreed to terms with the NFL's Rams than Cannon signed another deal with the AFL's Houston Oilers. It paid him twice the money.

What could cause such double dealing? A feeding frenzy for players in an ever-changing world of pro football in the sixties.

The primary question with Cannon was, Who would be the lucky team to take home the can't-miss superstar who would fit nicely in either league?

As the best-known prospect out of college that year, Cannon was drafted No. 1 overall in both leagues. He was the most visible player for the upstart AFL in its attempt to grab a chunk of the football market from the NFL.

It was a matter of anything goes. The deep-pocketed AFL owners had unlimited cash to make this a competitive battle for top college players.

So it became a time of litigation, double signings, and double dealing.

"There were a lot of shenanigans going on," said Jon Morris, a six-time AFL all-star with the Boston Patriots. "They were signing players before the draft. They were giving money to agents. As an offensive lineman, I wasn't part of that. But I heard some stories."

One of the stories was the case of Joe Don Looney, an Oklahoma fullback who signed with the New York Giants of the NFL. And with the Kansas City Chiefs (of the AFL). "I signed with both of them. I got bonuses from both of them. I cashed both their checks."

Litigation was sure to follow—for Morris, for Cannon, and for any of the new pros who were double dipping.

In Cannon's case, he was right in the middle of a very high-profile confrontation.

Few college football players have been more adored and idolized by their schools than Cannon, whose number 20 was retired immediately after his Heisman-winning season in 1959.

Cannon was the product of a blue-collar neighborhood in North Baton Rouge, Louisiana, where his father worked as a janitor. He starred in football and track in high school before establishing a commanding presence at LSU with his savage running ability.

From his halfback position, Cannon threw fear into opponents. One runback of a punt against archrival Mississippi in 1959 was the highlight of his college career and established a timeless legend at LSU. It was simply known as "The Run."

It came during a battle of top 10 teams, LSU No. 1 as the defending national champion, and Mississippi as No. 6.

A rare miscue by Cannon had allowed Mississippi to take a 3–0 lead late in the game. Cannon hoped to make up for his mistake as he dropped back to receive a punt. He stood at his five-yard line, hands on hips.

LSU coach Paul Dietzel had a rule against fielding punts inside the 15-yard line. But rules weren't Cannon's big thing.

"He just liked to run," noted the *Shreveport Times.*

The ball hit the turf. After a couple of bounces, Cannon gathered in the pigskin at the 11 and took off.

Cannon shrugged off a blow to the knees at his 19. Then he dragged a tackler 10 yards before shedding him.

Now he was at the 40 with a little more running room, then at the 50 and across midfield to Mississippi's 45.

Cannon evaded another tackler before finally breaking into the clear.

"When I saw Johnny Robinson looking back for someone to block, I felt this was it," Cannon later remembered of his backfield mate. "Just don't stub your toe, I told myself."

Cannon completed his run into the end zone, lifting LSU to a 7–3 victory.

Mississippi's Charlie Flowers, like Cannon an All-American, was on the field when the LSU star blew right by him on the way to the end zone.

"It was like a high school player trying to tackle an All-American," Flowers said. "He went through my hands like nothing."

The run sealed Cannon's Heisman selection, even though he had a subpar game against the same Mississippi team in the Sugar Bowl that season.

But other parts of his football life weren't so clear cut. Especially when he headed to the pros.

The Rams sought a court injunction to prevent Cannon from playing in the AFL.

"The Rams intend to enforce the contract," said Rams general manager Pete Rozelle—yes, THAT Pete Rozelle, soon to be the NFL commissioner.

A total of 425 players were taken in the first AFL draft in December 1959. Cannon was the most intriguing story.

He had signed that three-year deal with the Rams worth $50,000, then a small fortune. The Oilers came back and offered

Cannon even more riches: a contract that would make him football's first $100,000 player.

The money, said Cannon, "was too great to resist."

Meanwhile, other teams in the AFL dug deep down in their pockets as they went after the big names in college football. The battle was on with the NFL.

Four of five players on the All-America team signed with teams in the new league: Cannon with Houston, halfback Ron Burton with Boston, fullback Flowers with the Los Angeles Chargers, and quarterback Richie Lucas with Buffalo.

It was Cannon's double signing that overshadowed any other transaction.

That second signing was done with quite the dramatic flourish, too: in a symbolic gesture, Cannon staged his signing with the Oilers under the goalposts at the Sugar Bowl in New Orleans. No matter that LSU had just lost the game to Ole Miss, 21–0.

The NFL immediately filed suit against the Oilers and the AFL to void the signing of Cannon. Now a judge would have to decide which team he belonged to.

The ruling: victory for the AFL!

The court said Cannon's agreement with the Rams was illegal because he had yet to complete his college year when he signed.

"Cannon Now Is Free to Play with Oilers in New Loop," headlined the *New York Times*.

Cannon received a reported $20,000 signing bonus and $30,000 per year for three seasons for a total of $110,000. That wasn't all, according to some reports. The Oilers set up a string of health clubs with Cannon the nominal head, along with giving him a cut on profits from a group of service centers and a new car. It was the AFL's biggest win in the player battle with the NFL.

That war for players between the leagues went on in with all kinds of intrigue. There were the "babysitters." Teams would actually hide players in hotels and elsewhere so that the other league was unable to find them until after the draft.

It was helpful that one of the AFL's owners was Barron Hilton.

"The Hiltons, having all those hotels, were involved in trying to help all the AFL teams, and they got us rooms for the players," said Al Locasale, a longtime assistant to Raiders owner Al Davis. "We took Harry Schuh, a big tackle out of Memphis State, and Al hid him in Hawaii. The kid was asked where he wanted to go, and he said Hawaii."

Other teams didn't have to go that far to hide players.

Longtime NFL executive Joe Browne recalled, "After the first common draft, one of Pete (Rozelle's) friends, Jack Landry, a marketing guy for Marlboro who was one of the babysitters, came up to the stage. It was about 5:30 p.m. and Jack walked up to Pete on the podium and asked him, 'Pete, I got three Michigan State linebackers in a motel in Yonkers, what am I supposed to do?' Everybody cracked up."

Both leagues mostly went after the same players, although the AFL owners were quicker to discover talent in the small black colleges. The NFL did most of its recruiting in the major college conferences, which were mostly white.

"We competed for players, boy, did we," said Cleveland Browns owner Art Modell. "Yeah, everybody was hiding players—the Chiefs had Buck Buchanan, and he was no small fry; he was pretty difficult to hide. Ralph Wilson, one of the founders of the AFL, [was] one of my dearest friends. But he and I always seemed to be going after the same players, and he was a tough competitor, and I was. We just made it work."

But there was animosity from the NFL owners toward the new league. "Initially, the NFL owners did not want to merge," Browne said. "They were forced into it by the economics."

Both leagues were worried that a bidding war would drive up prices. They were right, and Cannon was an obvious example of that.

The Oilers seemed to have gotten it right with Cannon too. There were no complaints about his early performances on the field. In 1960 he scored on an 88-yard run to help the Oilers beat the Chargers for the AFL championship. The following season the Chargers moved to San Diego, with the same result. Once again, Cannon was in the middle of everything. He scored the only touchdown of the game as the Oilers clinched their second straight league title.

His 1961 season was classic Cannon. He led the league in rushing while putting together 2,043 all-purpose yards. In one memorable game against the New York Titans, Cannon scored five touchdowns.

The rest of Cannon's career was solid if not spectacular, ending in 1970 after 11 years playing for Houston, Oakland, and Kansas City. For some of that time, Cannon struggled with a back injury.

When one career finished, another started.

Cannon returned to his hometown of New Orleans and opened a thriving practice as an orthodontist. Thriving, that is, until the FBI showed up at his door.

To the shock and dismay of an entire community in which he had been a hero, Cannon was arrested for his participation in a $6 million counterfeiting ring. He was sentenced to a five-year prison term. While in prison, Cannon put his time to good use, helping the warden overhaul the clinic and provide good dental care for prisoners.

It was as memorable as any great play he made on the gridiron.

GIL BRANDT

Gil Brandt served as chief talent scout for the Dallas Cowboys' first 29 years of their existence (1960–1989), a period when they famously became known as "America's Team." He developed many of the scouting techniques used today by NFL teams, such as computer analysis of prospects, especially those from small colleges, and converting basketball players and track athletes into football players.

In addition he was one of the first scouts to look outside of American shores for football talent, particularly for kickers who had played soccer. Through the years, Brandt brought to Dallas such famous names as future Hall of Famers Bob Hayes, Roger Staubach, Bob Lilly, and Randy White, not to mention dozens of other gems such as Lee Roy Jordan and Ed "Too Tall" Jones.

Ask Brandt one question about his career and then sit back and receive a history lesson—no charge! (Read more about Gil Brandt in chapter 11.)

> When I was hired by the Cowboys, they were actually not in existence. We did not get a franchise until after the 1960 draft. Tex Schramm hired me on the premise we would get a franchise. At the time, Tex was in charge of sports programming at CBS.
>
> One of my jobs was finding free agents, guys that had not been drafted in the National Football League. The first guy that I signed was Jake Crouthamel, a running back at Dartmouth.
>
> The first time I went head to head with Crouthamel, he was an undrafted free agent. We paid him a flat $7,500. At the time, Tex remarked if we keep paying money like that we'll go broke. So I said, "Tex, he was the *first* choice of the LA Chargers [of the AFL]."
>
> The first year that the two leagues were competing for players was very mild. I don't think anybody had any money. Then in December

1961 we had the draft. Our first-round draft choice was Bob Lilly. We signed him for a $12,000 contract and a $4,000 bonus.

I told Tex I had done a good job. The Green Bay Packers paid Herb Adderley much more: $15,000 with a $5,000 bonus to sign.

It continued to escalate. The guy that got the most money, nobody talks about. It was when the Giants drafted Francis Peay in 1966. He got a huge signing bonus. It was a historic signing bonus and the start of something big. It was paid out as an annuity that was supposed to cost about $600,000. So we went from no signing bonus at the start of the 1960s to a $600,000 annuity.

That was one of the things that the two sides realized: you didn't get rich by spending money foolishly.

It was a league of haves and have-nots. It didn't make a difference if it was the NFL or AFL. Some owners and franchises had a better chance to succeed financially than others. As an example, Denver was a franchise known as good sports people but didn't have a lot of cash. There was a big disparity in the league as far as gate receipts were concerned. We played to a full house in Green Bay, and we got a $300,000 check. In New York, you got a million-dollar check. There was a lot of difference in league cities.

The Chicago Bears and New York Giants were two of the teams that separated themselves from the rest. The Dumont Network went to the Bears and Giants and gave them $200,000 apiece for their TV rights. They realized if they got the TV money there was no way some teams like Green Bay and Cleveland could compete with them.

The NFL thought the AFL would go away, but they had the staying power.

Ralph Wilson [owner of the Buffalo Bills], gave money to other teams so they could compete. It was a lot of hard work, and [it took] brilliant people at all levels to become successful after floundering.

Our battle for players with the AFL featured the so-called babysitters who would hide players so the other league couldn't find them. There was a group of people, ex-coaches, ex-players, even the governor of Oregon, who were involved.

I did all the signing for the Cowboys. And I tried to develop a personal relationship with the players.

In the early 1960s, I would spend the summer going to Cincinnati, or Chicago, and formed a relationship with someone among the top 50 players. When it came time to draft, you knew who he was and he knew who you were. We did very well signing players.

6

A DRAFT GENIUS
AND THREE WISE MEN

When Jimmy Johnson replaced the Dallas legend Tom Landry as the Cowboys' coach, many NFL insiders scoffed at the notion that a college-trained coach with no pro experience could handle the challenge. They cited Landry's superb record as the only man to lead the team since its inception in 1960 until the changeover in 1989.

Johnson, the critics said, would soon get his comeuppance, on and off the field, and would then scoot back to school, where he belonged.

Then Johnson settled in for his first draft, and while team owner Jerry Jones was the official general manager and has often taken credit for the selections, it was Johnson's expertise that would carry the day—and the next few years.

"The time I was with the team, I had complete and total responsibility over the football operation," Johnson told the *Dallas Morning News*. "That meant personnel, the draft, coaches, including the strength coach. Everything. It was always in my contract."

Johnson coached the Cowboys from 1989 until he left in a dispute with Jones after the 1993 season. Johnson was responsible in '89 alone for such picks as Troy Aikman, Steve Wisniewski (a star with the Raiders, not the Cowboys), Daryl Johnston, Mark Stepnoski, Tony Tolbert, and Keith Jennings (who became a regular with the Bears).

Aikman simply became a Hall of Famer, leading Dallas to three Super Bowl titles in four years. Johnston was a star fullback as adept at blocking as in catching passes, a strong locker room presence, and a key to Emmitt Smith's success. Stepnoski was a five-time Pro Bowl center and one of the most important blockers for Smith and protectors of Aikman. Tolbert had 57 sacks during the 1990s, tops of any Dallas player.

Johnson also grabbed another quarterback, Steve Walsh—who played for him with the Miami Hurricanes and who, many say, was Johnson's preference over Aikman at the outset. The Walsh pick came in the supplementary draft and cost the Cowboys the top overall spot in 1990.

Walsh would spend 11 seasons with six NFL teams—can you say journeyman? He even started five games for Dallas before Aikman took charge of the job for the next decade. There was even some thought that Johnson felt Walsh was the superior prospect. Johnson used Walsh as his starter in spots during that initial season with the Cowboys, but that was as much to protect Aikman's well-being on a team that would win one game as it was a vote of confidence in Walsh. A 0–4 start and a broken finger for Aikman were minor setbacks, it turned out.

Of course, Johnson was just getting started. And the real coup came in the most significant trade involving picks in draft history when he sent star running back Herschel Walker to the Vikings.

That the deal took place in midseason of 1989 was strange enough; huge NFL trades are as rare as a smile from Bill Belichick.

That the Cowboys would not actually use most of the selections they got from Minnesota for Walker—Johnson would wheel and deal many of those—certainly complicated the equation.

That Johnson would build a minidynasty in Big D thanks to the trade was pure genius.

Trade talks were initiated by Vikings general manager Mike Lynn, who approached Johnson during training camp. Lynn believed the Vikings, who were 11–5 in 1988, might be one difference maker away from a championship. He targeted Walker.

"I might be interested in that Herschel Walker guy," Lynn said.

But Johnson scoffed. "That's the only Pro Bowl player that we've got," he replied.

But when Dallas began losing game after game, Johnson recognized an opportunity. He would turn it into the steal of the century.

First, though, Cleveland had joined the party and sought the 27-year-old Walker. The Browns couldn't meet the steep price Johnson had placed on the running back, however: picks in each of the first three rounds, spread over a number of years.

Lynn had a counteroffer: Dallas could have five players, each with a first-round, second-round, or third-round pick attached.

Ever the negotiator, Johnson wanted another first-rounder.

Lynn bit.

"That's why at the press conference I said, 'This is a great train robbery,'" Johnson told the Associated Press. "Everybody looked at me like I was a complete fool, including Jerry, because they weren't sure we could pull this thing off."

What Johnson was really pulling off wasn't quite clear when the '89 season ended with the Cowboys at 1–15—but minus a 1990 first-rounder of their own, which was surrendered for Walsh.

Johnson infuriated Lynn when he told him the Cowboys would not keep any of the players—Jesse Solomon, David Howard, Issiac Holt, Darrin Nelson (who never reported to Dallas and was dealt instead to San Diego), and Alex Stewart. The Cowboys actually held on to cornerback Holt, who won a Super Bowl with them, through 1992. Howard spent one and a half seasons with the Cowboys, as did Solomon. Stewart was waived.

Johnson's motives were simple: collect draft picks. Then barter those for more picks.

Two months after the Cowboys' last-place finish and Minnesota's elimination in the divisional round of the 1989 playoffs, the rest of the Walker transaction was completed. Eighteen players would be involved, the biggest trade in NFL draft history.

And Jimmy really went to work. What he had in hand was ammunition to go after the guys he felt would lift Dallas from also-ran to elite once more.

Like Johnson, team owner Jones was a bit of a gambler. If nothing else, the trade established how aggressive the new regime in Dallas would be. "I've had times in my life when I wouldn't take risks because if I lost, I would've busted," Jones said. "When you have the dynamic of a pocket full of picks, you can gamble. . . . As much as the picks themselves brought us players, that attitude of risk-taking made a big difference in how we built the team."

Now that Dallas had this boatload of draft picks, the key was to use them correctly. Johnson wound up making 51 trades in his five seasons coaching the Cowboys.

Most significantly, in 1990 he moved up from 21st to 17th, initially seeking James Francis, a linebacker from Baylor. But the Bengals grabbed Francis, and Johnson turned his attention to a running back from Florida, Emmitt Smith.

Here, Johnson lucked out because the '90 grab bag was the first allowing underclassmen into the draft if their high school class had completed its junior year at college.

"Emmitt was ready for the NFL," Johnson said, "and we knew he could be one of the main (building) blocks for the Cowboys. You would hear how he couldn't outrun people or didn't hit the hole fast enough or wasn't big enough (5–10, 220). Well, Emmitt was ready, and I think he proved it a few times."

Sure did. Like becoming Offensive Rookie of the Year, then a league and Super Bowl MVP, followed by the career-rushing record and a trip to the Hall of Fame.

Yet the Cowboys' 1990 draft, the first after the Walker trade, paled in comparison to what Johnson and Jones achieved in 1989—and again in 1991.

Smith was the only star to come out of the 1990 group, although defensive tackle (DT) Jimmie Jones was solid during his four seasons in Big D, and defensive back (DB) Kenneth Gant won two Super Bowls as a Cowboy.

Where the Walker deal made its most impact was over the next two years. The likes of Darren Woodson, Russell Maryland, Kevin Smith, Dixon Edwards, Godfrey Myles, and Clayton Holmes wound up in Dallas as Johnson swapped selections like it was fantasy football.

Most intriguing were the machinations to get the top overall spot in '91, with which he landed Maryland, whom Johnson had recruited to Miami years earlier.

Sensing the Patriots would be awful in 1990, Johnson targeted them for a potential trade well before the season ended. Before the draft in April, he gave up a first-round pick and a second-rounder, plus three veterans—one of them his starting middle linebacker Eugene Lockhart—to get the top choice.

Johnson wanted Notre Dame's Raghib "Rocket" Ismail to pair with Michael Irvin, the receiver Dallas took in the 11th slot in 1988, the year before the JJs arrived. But Ismail chose to sign with the Canadian Football League's (CFL) Toronto Argonauts, getting nearly $30 million, a figure Jones and Johnson scoffed at.

Ironically, Ismail would complete his pro career with the Cowboys for three seasons, long after Johnson had split.

With Ismail headed to the Great White North, Johnson turned his attention to the 300-pound defensive tackle he brought to the Hurricanes before leaving for the NFL.

"I guess I was one of his boys," Maryland said. "And he left an indelible mark on the Cowboys." Not to mention on the entire draft process. Maryland wound up playing 10 pro seasons, winning three Super Bowls, making a Pro Bowl, and epitomizing the brilliance of Johnson's drafting maneuvers.

And Maryland was just the first of a handful of key Cowboys from the '91 class. Alvin Harper, Kelvin Pritchett, Leon Lett, and Larry Brown came to Dallas that year. All were significant contributors to the championship run, with Brown taking Super Bowl most valuable player (MVP) honors in the 1996 win over Pittsburgh.

The impact of the Walker trade was felt in 1992 as well. Nine months before Dallas would beat Buffalo for the NFL crown, Johnson was adding Kevin Smith, Robert Jones, Woodson, and Holmes to the mix. All of them earned Super Bowl rings.

Johnson did make some errors in his relatively short stint with America's Team. Second-rounder Jimmy Smith, a receiver from Jackson State, lasted only seven games in 1992 in Dallas. He wound up as the Jaguars' greatest pass catcher, although he also had major off-field issues.

Johnson eventually coached the Miami Dolphins, where his drafting record was spotty. For every outstanding pick—linebacker (LB) Zach Thomas, 154th overall in 1996; and defensive end (DE) Jason Taylor, 73rd in 1997—there also were the Yatil Greens (first round, '97), John Averys (first round, '98), and J. J. Johnsons (second round, '99).

Meanwhile, Walker, who received a $1.25 million bonus from Jones to ensure he would report to the Vikings in October 1989, did little in Minnesota and was gone by 1992. So was Lynn, vilified by Vikings fans for years to come.

Rather than being hated by Cowboys fans for his abrupt departure in '94, Johnson has been missed like the movie star who escapes your clutches just before the big kiss. Dallas won the 1995 NFL title, its third in four seasons, with the roster Johnson built but that his archrival Barry Switzer coached. It hasn't come close to a championship since.

After his mediocre four-season stay with the Dolphins, Johnson has never gone back to coaching. He's been a fixture on Fox television's NFL studio shows and has enjoyed the good life in the Florida Keys.

Regrets? With apologies to Old Blue Eyes (Sinatra, not Johnson), he's had a few but, then again, too few to mention.

"I think I proved them wrong," he once said. "I'm having a heck of a time, and I'm going to Cancún fishing . . ."

SMART MEN

Some of the NFL's most successful coaches were also masters of the draft. Here's a look at three and the magic they weaved.

Chuck Noll

When Noll took over the Steelers in 1969, they had never been to the playoffs. NEVER!

After going 1–13 that season, nothing was further from realization in Pittsburgh than a lineup loaded with future Hall of Famers and nearly a fistful of Super Bowl rings.

But Noll and his staff of scouts would scour the nation unlike any previous Steelers regime, looking everywhere from their backyard at Pitt to the Division III ranks to the historically black colleges. And they would strike bull's-eye after bull's-eye.

One day after Noll was hired, the Steelers drafted Joe Greene from North Texas State—hardly a powerhouse in the football-rich Lone Star State. Greene was merely the first of nine draftees who would make the Canton shrine after being selected in the Noll era. The others were Terry Bradshaw, Mel Blount, Jack Ham, Franco Harris, Jack Lambert, Lynn Swann, John Stallworth, and Mike Webster.

Incredibly, four eventual Hall of Famers landed in Pittsburgh in the 1974 draft: wide receivers (WRs) Swann (first round) and Stallworth (fourth); middle linebacker Lambert (second); and center Webster (fifth).

Leave out the Hall of Famers and the Steelers still had some superb choices as they built the Steel Curtain defense and an offense that went from among the most powerful ground games to among the most dynamic passing attacks of its time.

Consider the following in 1971: DE Dwight White, WR Frank Lewis, DT Ernie Holmes, offensive tackle (OT) Larry Brown, offensive guard (OG) Gerry Mullins, and safety (S) Mike Wagner. All significant parts of title teams.

And in 1972 came DT Steve Furness, OT Gord Gravelle, and LB Ed Bradley. In 1973, it was cornerback (CB) J. T. Thomas and LB Loren Toews.

Each of them earned championship hardware along with the big stars.

"He was one of the great coaches of the game," Steelers owner Dan Rooney once said of Noll. "He ranks up there with [George] Halas, [Tom] Landry, and [Curly] Lambeau."

At the draft table, Noll might have been better than all of those fellow Hall of Famers.

Bill Walsh

Like Noll, Walsh inherited a franchise that had never reached the top of the NFL, although at least the 49ers had been to the playoffs.

Walsh took over in 1979, 10 years after Noll was hired by the Steelers. And just like Noll, Walsh's first team was abysmal, going 2–14.

Walsh emulated Noll's commitment to the draft and was helped in personnel evaluation by having coached Stanford the previous two seasons before the Niners hired him.

While Walsh became practically exalted for popularizing the West Coast offense, it was basically a variation of other attacks that such coaching greats as Paul Brown and Sid Gillman had used. Perhaps Walsh should be just as celebrated for his skill at the draft, helped greatly by the freedom he was afforded by owner Eddie DeBartolo Jr., and by the able assistance of front-office wiz Carmen Policy.

In 1979, Walsh went searching for two foundation pieces: a quality quarterback with smarts and leadership skills, and a clutch receiver for him to throw to.

Bingo: Joe Montana and Dwight Clark. Neither of them a first-rounder.

Walsh ignored the criticism that Montana didn't have a strong arm and was not tough enough to take a pounding. What he saw was the perfect maestro for his offense, a passer with touch, a quick release, great feet, and a great mind.

"Some people look at what a player can't do," Walsh once said, "instead of what he can do well. Joe could do everything we wanted and do it very well."

The next year, Walsh added LBs Keena Turner and Bobby Leopold, running back (RB) Earl Cooper, and DE Jim Stuckey. He followed that with three defensive backs in his first four selections in 1981, including Ronnie Lott, who would play cornerback and safety and be the 49ers' defensive leader for a decade on his way to the Hall of Fame.

"The importance of a player like Ronnie to any team can't be overestimated," Walsh said. "You win championships with players like Ronnie Lott."

That year, with rookies Lott, Carlton Williamson, and Eric Wright in the secondary, San Francisco won its first Super Bowl. It was also the season of "The Catch"—Montana to Clark to win the National Football Conference (NFC) crown.

In succeeding years, Walsh would draft RB Roger Craig, LB Riki Ellison, S Tom Holmoe, center (C) Jess Sapolu, OG Guy McIntyre, nose tackle (NT) Michael Carter, and, oh yeah, some wideout from Mississippi Valley State named Jerry Rice.

By the time Rice, merely the greatest pass catcher the game has seen, was selected 16th overall in 1985, the 49ers had won two championships. Yet Walsh had not had his best draft crop.

That came in '86: DE Charles Haley (fourth round), WR John Taylor (third), fullback (FB) Tom Rathman (third), OT Steve Wallace (fourth), CBs Don Griffin (sixth), and Tim McKyer (third).

Under Walsh's watch the 49ers won three Super Bowls in eight seasons and another after he turned the coaching reins over to George Seifert. Walsh was such a phenomenal success because he stuck to his draft philosophy that evaluating players is not a science.

"It must take into account a myriad of factors," he once told SportsXchange, "and, in the final analysis, must answer one critical question: Can this man perform on my team?"

If Walsh picked him, he almost certainly could.

Paul Brown

Both Walsh and Noll, plus all-time coaching victories leader Don Shula, were disciples of Paul Brown, who founded the Cleveland Browns in the All-America Football Conference, which they dominated. Brown then brought his franchise into the NFL—and still dominated.

After he was unceremoniously dumped as coach in Cleveland, he started up the Cincinnati Bengals.

Brown has been credited with many pro football innovations, including developing playbooks and game plans; hiring a staff of full-time assistants; using film clips to analyze player performance; and calling plays from the sideline.

Oh, he also was pretty good at this drafting thing.

Although he brought a veteran-laden team into the NFL in 1950, Brown understood the machinations of the draft as well as anyone. He supplemented the likes of Otto Graham, Dante Lavelli, and Bill Willis with a bevy of formidable players, and through the years his expert picks included WR Bobby Mitchell; RB-WRs Ray Renfro and Preston Carpenter; DEs Doug Atkins (who became a star with the Bears), Willie Davis (later a Hall of Famer with the Packers) and Paul Wiggin; LBs Galen Fiss and Walt Michaels; CBs Bernie Parrish and Jim Shofner; S Ken Konz; OGs John Wooten and Jim Ray Smith; and OT Dick Schafrath.

That was just in the 1950s, and the list ignores the most impressive and important draft in the illustrious history of the Brown-led Browns. In 1957, Paul Brown added to his roster quarterback Milt Plum in the second round, DT Henry Jordan (a future standout in Green Bay) in the fifth, and offensive guard Gene Hickerson—yet another Canton-bound player—in the seventh. And some guy named Jim Brown with the sixth overall choice.

Nine future Hall of Famers were selected in that 1957 crop: Brown, Paul Hornung, Len Dawson, Sonny Jurgensen, Jim Parker, Tommy MacDonald, Jordan, Hickerson, and Don Maynard. Three went to the same team. Paul Brown's team.

In Jim Brown, Paul Brown saw every component for greatness. As he said years later, "As a pure runner, Jim Brown was the best ever. He had a combination of power, intense speed, and a shuffling foot action that made it difficult to stop him. Jim rarely fumbled, was tireless, intimidating at times, and his durability was unusual."

Yet five teams passed on the running back out of Syracuse who, a half century after he prematurely retired to become an actor, still is considered by many the greatest football player the NFL has seen.

Paul Brown knew better than to make a similar mistake and let Jim Brown go elsewhere.

NOT-SO-SMART MEN

For all the draft-day deftness of the Johnsons, Nolls, Walshes, and Browns, there have been some moves that can only be described as D-U-M-B.

Head-scratching, eye-rolling, fist-pounding dumb.

Here are three of the most infamous decisions in NFL draft history.

Everything for Ricky

Mike Ditka has been enamored of many things in his career, not the least of which are a good cigar and a great running back.

Stogie in hand, Ditka pulled off one of the most noteworthy and confounding transactions ever in 1999 to get that super back: Ricky Williams.

While the top three teams were diving headfirst for quarter-backs—Tim Couch to expansion Cleveland, Donovan McNabb to Philadelphia, and Akili Smith to Cincinnati—Ditka was angling for a shot at the Texas powerhouse and Heisman Trophy winner. He wanted to get up to the fourth overall slot from No. 12 that his Saints owned, but Indianapolis GM Bill Polian had other ideas.

Polian wanted to pair a dynamic running back with Peyton Manning, and he was going to stay at No. 4 and take that player.

It just wasn't Williams he wanted, it was Edgerrin James of the University of Miami.

Indianapolis took James, and Ditka was ready to light up, because he'd worked a deal with Washington to get to the fifth spot if Williams remained on the board. The price?

How about the Saints' choices at Nos. 12, 71, 107, 144, 179, and 218? Yep, the whole caboodle. Plus two picks in the 2000 draft.

Actually, Ditka had said weeks earlier he would be willing to trade all of his picks for Williams, so he entered the draft with no hole cards.

Washington eventually dealt away some of those picks, but it also got the best player of any chosen in those spots, cornerback Champ Bailey.

Ditka wore a Rastafarian wig when he introduced Williams to the New Orleans media. Williams later wore a wedding dress for a cover photo with Ditka on a national magazine.

A decade later, Ditka told the *Chicago Sun-Times* he still believed it was the right move.

"You'll never find a better guy, a sweetheart of a guy, a personable guy, a guy who tries to do the right things, and I think his teammates see that," he said of Williams, who by 2010 was in his penultimate pro season, having played only three years for the Saints.

"Now you could argue, if you want to: Did we give up too much to get him? Maybe," Ditka added. "But if you want somebody, why not give it up? And the other reason we wanted him—I wanted him—was that they needed somebody to market in New Orleans and I thought he would be great."

Off to Canada

Seeking a playmaker for its defense, the Bills focused their attention on Tom Cousineau of Ohio State in the 1979 draft.

Buffalo owned the first and fifth spots in the opening round. The Bills had gotten the top pick not by being the worst team in football—San Francisco owned that, uh, distinction with a 2–14 record—but by having dealt their biggest star, O. J. Simpson, to the 49ers.

As the legend goes, the Bills were all set to grab Cousineau with the first overall selection once he passed a physical in New York, the site of the draft. He passed, returned to his hotel, and was told the Bills would pick him up for dinner.

"I was waiting at the hotel and they never showed," Cousineau told AOL in 2010. "They never called. I'm not kidding. Hearing no or being turned down or snubbed was not a new experience, but it seemed . . . first of all very rude. And inhospitable."

Even worse, according to Cousineau's agent, Jimmy Walsh— yes, the same guy who guided Joe Namath's career—it meant the Bills really weren't all that interested in Cousineau.

The Canadian Football League was because Cousineau had some French-Canadian blood. What a coup if a CFL team could sign the top pick in the NFL draft!

Without the Bills being clued in, Walsh and Montreal Alouettes owner Sam Berger began quiet and quick negotiations on a deal. On draft day, Cousineau had an offer for more than $1 million for three years.

Buffalo still took Cousineau to begin the proceedings, but its offer of $1.2 million over five years didn't exceed or even match Berger's bid.

Voilà: Cousineau was an Alouette.

"Going to Canada was never my first choice," Cousineau said. "And the Bills didn't have to match, but we told them, 'You need to do better. You know it and I know it.'"

Cousineau spent three years in Canada and then moved back to the NFL. Buffalo matched a deal he got with the Houston Oilers and then dealt him to Cleveland for a first-rounder in the 1983 draft.

And while the Bills totally miscalculated on Cousineau, they made up for it with that pick, which they used on Jim Kelly.

Bye-Bye Bus

When the Rams drafted Jerome Bettis with the 10th overall pick in 1993, they were hoping he would make their fans forget Eric Dickerson. Or at least that he would remind them of Dickerson because he would be posting similar rushing numbers.

Bettis was good enough to go to the Pro Bowl in each of his first two seasons in Los Angeles, rushing for 2,454 yards and 10 touchdowns in that span. He was the NFL's Offensive Rookie of the Year after leaving Notre Dame, and his outgoing personality made him one of the Rams' most popular players.

And when the team moved to St. Louis in 1995, well, the entire city could have been Bettis's realm.

But "The Bus" held out for a new contract, which he didn't get. He missed only the preseason, but he'd alienated Rams coach Rich Brooks.

"It was a frustrating season because I came in after a hold-out, and it was something that me and management were dealing with," Bettis told the *St. Louis Post-Dispatch*. "But Brooks held it against me as if I did something to him. . . . Each week he would pull me out of the football game after I performed fairly well. He would yank me. He did that the majority of the season until I hurt my foot."

As the draft approached, it was clear that Brooks and Rams vice president of football operations Steve Ortmayer were ready to rid themselves of Bettis.

How they did it couldn't have been more misguided.

Not only did St. Louis send Bettis to the Steelers along with a third-round pick for a second and a fourth, but also the Rams then selected Nebraska's Lawrence Phillips to replace Bettis in the backfield.

"The Bus" cruised to six straight 1,000-yard seasons in Pittsburgh, became a vocal leader in the locker room and the community, and capped his career with a Super Bowl title—in his hometown of Detroit, no less, in February 2006.

Phillips was a problem on and off the field from the get-go and wound up with a 30-year prison sentence for assault. He rushed for 1,453 yards in his fractured three pro seasons, fewer yards than Bettis gained in 1997 alone.

Brooks was fired after the '96 campaign. Ortmayer lost his position at the same time.

7

THE LISTS

NFL teams spend millions of dollars, and seemingly just as many hours, scouting and evaluating players. Sometimes they strike it rich early—13 top overall picks are in the Pro Football Hall of Fame.

Sometimes they hit the mother lode late—did someone say Tom Brady?

Here's a look at the bold and beautiful, the fantastics and the flops, in NFL draft history.

FRANCHISE BESTS AND WORSTS

Arizona Cardinals

Best Pick: Larry Wilson, S, Utah

The face of the franchise from 1960 to 1972, Wilson was the 74th pick in '60 and became the best safety in the game. Fearsome, he stood up to every challenge despite rarely being surrounded by much defensive talent and made the Hall of Fame in 1978.

Worst Pick: Wendell Bryant, DT, Wisconsin

Taken 12th overall in 2002, Bryant played in 29 games over three seasons and then was cut because of drug policy violations. He managed 28 tackles and 1½ sacks in his career.

Atlanta Falcons

Best Pick: Jeff Van Note, C, Kentucky

Something of an afterthought when chosen 262nd in 1969, Van Note parlayed strength, smarts, and dedication into an 18-season career with the Falcons. The anchor of their offensive line for a generation.

Worst Pick: Aundray Bruce, DE, Auburn

It's hard to pick someone who spent 11 seasons in the NFL. Bruce fits, though, because he started a mere 42 games and rarely was more than a backup with little impact despite being top overall selection in 1988.

Baltimore Ravens

Best Pick: Jonathan Ogden, OT, UCLA

Selected with the team's first-ever pick in 1996 after the move from Cleveland, Ogden was star left tackle through 2006 and made 11 Pro Bowls.

Worst Pick: Travis Taylor, WR, Florida

Projected to be dynamic deep threat, Taylor was the 10th overall choice in 2000, but battled injuries and did little in Baltimore.

Buffalo Bills

Best Pick: Bruce Smith, DE, Virginia Tech

Pro football's all-time sacks leader, the 1985 first overall pick was defensive leader for the team's four straight Super Bowl trips.

Worst Pick: Tom Cousineau, LB, Ohio State

Another top overall selection, he didn't even sign with Buffalo and went to the CFL. Eventually played seven NFL mediocre seasons elsewhere.

Carolina Panthers

Best Pick: Steve Smith, WR, Utah

A third-rounder in 2001, 74th overall, Smith brought a boulder-size chip on his short frame into the NFL. He parlayed his work ethic, intelligence, natural skills, and combativeness into a superb career.

Worst Pick: Rae Carruth, WR, Colorado

His speed was enticing, and the Panthers used the 27th overall spot in 1997 on Carruth. He played in 22 games with virtually no stats and later was convicted of conspiracy to commit murder, winding up in prison.

Chicago Bears

Best Pick: Richard Dent, DE, Tennessee State

If Chicago's defense of the 1980s was its best version of the Monsters of the Midway, it was because the Bears found Dent at the 203rd slot in 1983. A Super Bowl MVP, he pass-rushed his way right into the Hall of Fame.

Worst Pick: Cedric Benson, RB, Texas

In 2005, desperate for a ground game, the Bears used the fourth pick on Benson. He struggled, had off-field problems, and was released in 2008 after his second alcohol-related arrest in a month.

Cincinnati Bengals

Best Pick: Anthony Munoz, OT, Southern California

The greatest Bengal of them all, chosen third in 1980's first round, Munoz made 11 Pro Bowls on his way to the Hall of Fame.

Worst Pick: Ki-Jana Carter, RB, Penn State

Yet another player chosen to begin the draft, in 1995, Carter tore the ACL in his left knee on his third preseason carry. That was beginning of the end of a disappointing, injury-ravaged career.

Cleveland Browns

Best Pick: Jim Brown, RB, Syracuse

Who else but the greatest running back in football history? Brown went sixth in 1957 and rushed for 12,312 yards and 126 touchdowns before retiring at the peak of his career to pursue acting.

Worst Pick: Courtney Brown, DE, Penn State

How could a team mess up with a player of the same name? Courtney was no Jim Brown, for sure, and 2000's top overall choice was frequently sidelined by knee problems.

Dallas Cowboys

Best Pick: Emmitt Smith, RB, Florida

Considering the heist coach Jimmy Johnson pulled off in 1989 with the Herschel Walker trade, one of the picks Dallas got from Minnesota has to make this list. Easy choice: the NFL's career rushing leader, a three-time Super Bowl winner and one-time league MVP who made the Hall of Fame in 2010.

Worst Pick: Billy Cannon Jr., LB, Texas A&M

Why bloodlines don't matter in the draft. He was the son of 1959 Heisman Trophy winner Billy Cannon and went 25th overall in 1984. The younger Cannon appeared in eight games, got hurt, and never played again.

Denver Broncos

Best Pick: Shannon Sharpe, Tight End (TE), Savannah State

Deep in the 1990 draft, at selection 192, the Broncos took a shot with the younger brother of Packers receiver Sterling Sharpe. Shannon turned into one of the most prolific tight ends in NFL history and a Hall of Famer.

Worst Pick: Dick Butkus, LB, Illinois

Denver had no shot at signing the premier college linebacker in 1965; he was signed, sealed, and delivered for the Bears. Yet the Broncos used their top selection in the AFL grab bag on Butkus.

Detroit Lions

Best Pick: Joe Schmidt, LB, Pittsburgh

The greatest defensive player in Lions history, Schmidt was the 85th selection in 1953. He tore up opponents for most of his 13 seasons, was the linchpin of Detroit's 1957 title team, and was elected to the Hall of Fame in 1973.

Worst Pick: Charles Rogers, WR, Michigan State

The second pick in 2003 got off to a rousing start with two touchdowns (TDs) in his first game. Then came injuries, off-field issues, and NFL suspensions.

Green Bay Packers

Best Pick: Bart Starr, QB, Alabama

Some would opt for Aaron Rodgers, but while he slipped big-time in 2005, he still went in the opening round. It took 200 picks for Starr to be drafted, and all he did was take the Packers to five championships on his way to the Hall of Fame.

Worst Pick: Tony Mandarich, OT, Michigan State

Ballyhooed as the best blocking prospect in decades, Mandarich became the poster boy for steroid use and a failed career. Taken second to Troy Aikman in 1989—and directly ahead of Barry Sanders, Derrick Thomas, and Deion Sanders.

Houston Texans

Best Pick: Owen Daniels, TE, Wisconsin

Houston's offense was a one-man show (WR Andre Johnson) until this fourth-rounder, 98th overall in 2006, brought balance and some big plays.

Worst Pick: Travis Johnson, DT, Florida State

Rarely healthy and never a major contributor, this 2005 first-rounder had only two sacks in four seasons.

Indianapolis Colts

Best Pick: Peyton Manning, QB, Tennessee

Five MVP awards, all sorts of passing records, and an icon in a game of superstars, the 1998 top selection is one of the NFL's greatest players, regardless of era.

Worst Pick: Trev Alberts, LB, Nebraska

A college phenom who never showed much in the pros after going fifth overall in 1994.

Jacksonville Jaguars

Best Pick: Maurice Jones-Drew, RB, UCLA

Taken 60th overall in 2006, Jones-Drew became the only real offensive weapon for the Jaguars, leading the league in rushing in 2011. He made three Pro Bowls as a Jaguar.

Worst Pick: Blaine Gabbert, QB, Missouri

During the not-so-great quarterback rush of 2011, he was chosen 10th overall. He played more like a 10th-round pick and lasted an underwhelming three seasons in Jacksonville.

Kansas City Chiefs

Best Pick: Willie Lanier, LB, Morgan State

Not many linebackers from historically black universities made it big in the pros in the 1960s. The Chiefs went for Lanier with the 50th pick, and he paid them back by leading a championship defense and making the Hall of Fame.

Worst Pick: Todd Blackledge, QB, Penn State

The 1983 draft was rich as a gold mine in quarterbacks, but the Chiefs didn't hit pay dirt with Blackledge, the first player drafted by first-year coach John Mackovic. The seventh overall selection, Blackledge made his most impact as a broadcaster.

Miami Dolphins

Best Pick: Dan Marino, QB, Pittsburgh

How many teams were kicking themselves for years over passing on the prolific arm of Marino in 1983? The last of six quarterbacks (QBs) chosen in the opening round, he went 27th, became a starter as a rookie, led the Dolphins to the Super Bowl in 1984, and was the top passer in NFL history when he retired after the '99 season before heading to the Hall of Fame in 2005.

Worst Pick: Eric Kumerow, DE, Ohio State

The 16th pick in 1988 spent three unproductive seasons in the NFL.

Minnesota Vikings

Best Pick: John Randle, DT, Texas A&M–Kingsville

This might be cheating because he went undrafted in 1990, was signed by Minnesota, and had a Hall of Fame career. Randle finished with 137½ sacks, incredible for a tackle.

Worst Pick: Dimitrius Underwood, DE, Michigan State

Selected 29th overall in 1999, Underwood didn't last one day of training camp, dealing with mental illness issues.

New England Patriots

Best Pick: Tom Brady, QB, Michigan

Duh! All Brady did after going 199th in 2000 was guide the Patriots to the NFL title in his second pro season, win three Super Bowls in four years, and quarterback the team to a perfect 2007 regular season.

Worst Pick: Kenneth Sims, DE, Texas

The first choice in 1982 was never healthy in the NFL and managed to play only 74 games in eight seasons with Patriots. He had just 16 sacks, and the Patriots released him in 1990 after he reported out of shape.

New Orleans Saints

Best Pick: Marques Colston, WR, Hofstra

Near the end of 2006 draft, New Orleans took a chance on a rangy wideout with a history of drops. Selected 252nd, Colston has been this franchise's best receiver and a Super Bowl winner.

Worst Pick: Russell Erxleben, Placekicker–Punter (PK-P), Texas

New Orleans had the guts to go for a kicker with the 11th selection in 1979. Erxleben flopped as a punter—net punting average never exceeded 35.2 yards for a season—and rarely placekicked.

New York Giants

Best Pick: Lawrence Taylor, LB, North Carolina

The Giants held their breath as the Saints picked first, hoping they wouldn't grab Taylor. They took George Rogers, and New York never hesitated to add this prototype for the modern linebacker. Taylor was NFL MVP in 1986 and three-time Defensive Player of the Year (1981, 1982, and 1986).

Worst Pick: Rocky Thompson, RB, West Texas State

Thompson was fast and not much else. Chosen 17th overall in 1971 when some projected him to go in the third round, he did virtually nothing in two-plus years in New York.

New York Jets

Best Pick: Wayne Chrebet, WR, Hofstra

Cheating again, because like Minnesota's Randle, Chrebet was undrafted. He caught the coaches' eyes in 1995 because the

Jets trained at Hofstra, and Chrebet lasted a decade as an effective slot receiver.

Worst Pick: Blair Thomas, RB, Penn State

A bundle of talent, the 1990 second overall pick could never stay healthy. He managed barely over 2,000 yards rushing in four seasons with the Jets.

Oakland Raiders

Best Pick: Jim Otto, C, Miami

Not a bad way to start a franchise, Otto went in the 24th round in 1960 in first year of the AFL. He merely became that league's best center and a Hall of Famer.

Worst Pick: JaMarcus Russell, QB, LSU

Quite likely the worst pick in draft history—for any team—the 2007 top overall choice got paid more than $39 million before being cut after three seasons. Stats? He won only 7 of 25 starts, threw 23 interceptions, lost 15 fumbles, completed 52.1 percent of his passes, and had a passer rating of 65.2.

Philadelphia Eagles

Best Pick: Lou Creekmur, Offensive/Defensive Lineman (OL-DL), William and Mary

Philly made a brilliant pick at 243rd overall with the versatile Creekmur. Only problem: he went on to a Hall of Fame career with the Lions, never suiting up for the Eagles. He pursued a master's degree rather than joining Philadelphia in 1948, wound up in a frozen player pool in 1950, and was grabbed by Detroit.

Worst Pick: Kevin Allen, OT, Indiana

Allen's moment in the NFL—the 1985 season—was unmemorable; then he tested positive for cocaine at training camp, was charged with sexual assault, and spent three years in prison.

Pittsburgh Steelers

Best Pick: Terry Bradshaw, QB, Louisiana Tech

The top overall pick in 1970, Bradshaw became the first quarterback to win four Super Bowls and was MVP in two of them.

Worst Pick: Huey Richardson, LB, Florida

Taken 15th in 1991, Richardson played in only five games for the Steelers. Traded to Washington the following off-season, he was out of the NFL after two years.

St. Louis Rams

Best Pick: Deacon Jones, DE, Mississippi Valley State

The man the term "sack" was invented for lasted until the 186th pick in 1961, in great part because of where he went to college. Jones then became the most fearsome pass rusher in the game, the anchor of the Fearsome Foursome, and a Hall of Famer.

Worst Pick: Lawrence Phillips, RB, Nebraska

Trouble followed Phillips in his college and short pro careers. The Rams gambled on him in 1996 in the sixth overall spot, he was cut for insubordination in 1997, and eventually wound up in prison.

San Diego Chargers

Best Pick: Dan Fouts, QB, Oregon

Coach Don Coryell's high-powered passing attack needed a triggerman, and the Chargers found one in 1973 with the 64th overall pick. Fouts wound up a Hall of Famer and one of the NFL's most prolific passers.

Worst Pick: Ryan Leaf, QB, Washington State

Hard to believe Leaf was rated Peyton Manning's equal in 1998. One pick after Manning led off the draft by going to Indianapolis, Leaf was chosen. The Chargers soon regretted it: Leaf was immature and lacked dedication and a solid work ethic.

San Francisco 49ers

Best Pick: Joe Montana, QB, Notre Dame

Few franchises can boast such a rich draft history, and four-time Super Bowl champ Montana is the shiniest jewel. Chosen 82nd overall in 1979, he soon had the Niners winning titles, was being proclaimed the best quarterback of his era, and was headed for the Hall of Fame.

Worst Pick: Jim Druckenmiller, QB, Virginia Tech

Stick with the QBs, this time for a flop. Druckenmiller made one start in two seasons after going 26th overall in 1997, one of only three picks for San Francisco that year. His passer rating was an almost invisible 29.2.

Seattle Seahawks

Best Pick: Richard Sherman, CB, Stanford

Taken in the fifth round (154th overall), Sherman became an All-Pro and keyed Seattle's 2013 championship team with his aggressive, intelligent work.

Worst Pick: Steve Niehaus, DT, Notre Dame

Taken second overall in 1976, he played just 36 games with little impact for the new franchise.

Tampa Bay Buccaneers

Best Pick: Lee Roy Selmon, DE, Oklahoma

Some would argue for fellow Hall of Famers Derrick Brooks and Warren Sapp, but Selmon overcame an early losing culture in Tampa to turn things around with his versatility, leadership, and style.

Worst Pick: Eric Curry, DE, Alabama

Using the sixth overall spot in 1993, the Bucs thought they were getting a penetrating pass rusher. Curry managed all of 12 sacks in five years in Tampa.

Tennessee Titans/Houston Oilers

Best Pick: Earl Campbell, RB, Texas

Desperate to get the Heisman Trophy winner and Lone Star State superstar, the Oilers traded three picks and tight end Jimmie Giles to Tampa Bay for the top spot in 1978. Campbell soon was headed to the Hall of Fame.

Worst Pick: Adam "Pacman" Jones, DB, West Virginia

Although Jones eventually found a role on other teams, he was a bust for a 2005 sixth pick overall. Nonfootball issues plagued him in Tennessee.

Washington Redskins

Best Pick: Wayne Millner, End (E), Notre Dame

Selected in the eighth round in 1936, Millner was among the most accomplished receivers in the league during his 76-game career. He helped Washington win the 1937 title and was inducted into the Hall of Fame in 1968.

Worst Pick: Andre Johnson, OT, Penn State

This storied franchise would like to forget the 30th overall pick in 1996. The Redskins even traded up for him; he never got on the field as a rookie and was cut in 1997.

POSITION BESTS AND WORSTS

Five Best QB Picks

1. Tom Brady, 2000. Maybe the best choice at any position, Brady went from 199th selection to Super Bowl champion in two seasons. He added two more NFL titles before he was 28.
2. Joe Montana, 1979. Third-rounder (82nd overall) who immediately mastered San Francisco's West Coast offense, Montana led the Niners to four Super Bowl wins.
3. Roger Staubach, 1964. Dallas knew he would have to serve in the navy and spent only a 10th-round pick on its greatest quarterback.
4. Dan Marino, 1983. Six quarterbacks go in the first round, and he's the sixth. Miami was forever thankful for that.
5. Peyton Manning, 1998. The Colts chose correctly between Manning and Ryan Leaf, and Peyton became an all-time great.

Five Worst QB Picks

1. JaMarcus Russell, 2007. The Raiders loved his size and arm strength. Russell didn't love football and is an all-time biggest bust as top QB selection.
2. Tim Couch, 1999. The very first player the Browns drafted when they returned to the NFL. By midseason, Cleveland wanted another QB.
3. Terry Baker, 1963. The Rams went for a Heisman Trophy winner from Oregon State. Baker never fit and had one start in three pro seasons.
4. Randy Duncan, 1959. This Iowa QB was a college football Hall of Famer. As a top overall pick by the Packers, he headed to the CFL for more money and eventually became a lawyer.

5. Bobby Garrett, 1954. When the powerful Browns won a lottery for the top pick, they chose this Stanford stand-out. Garrett was called to active duty during Korean War and then traded to the Packers, where he played one season.

Five Best RB Picks

1. Leroy Kelly, 1964. Cleveland already had Jim Brown, so picking Kelly in the eighth round seemed to mean little. Then Brown walked away from football in 1965 and Kelly became an all-time bargain.
2. Jim Taylor, 1958. The Packers already had Paul Hornung when they took Taylor from LSU in the second round. That combo led Green Bay to the top, and both made the Hall of Fame.
3. Terrell Davis, 1995. An afterthought as the 196th selection, Davis wasn't a star at Georgia. He was exactly what the Broncos needed to finally win the Super Bowl.
4. Thurman Thomas, 1988. Questions about his knees and size dropped Thomas—who started ahead of Barry Sanders at Oklahoma State—to 40th overall. Buffalo grabbed him, and he helped the Bills to four straight American Football Conference (AFC) crowns.
5. Curtis Martin, 1995. New England took Martin with the 74th pick and he wound up Offensive Rookie of the Year, rushed for 1,000 yards in his first 10 seasons, and made the Hall of Fame as a Jet.

Five Worst RB Picks

1. Jay Berwanger, 1936. The first pick in the initial NFL draft, Berwanger took his Heisman Trophy and said no to the Eagles, who selected him, and to the Bears, who

traded for him. Not enough money in the pro game, Berwanger decided.

2. Tom Harmon, 1941. The Bears tried again, using the top spot on number 98, one of college football's greatest backs. Harmon lasted two seasons with the Rams after World War II, in which he won a Silver Star and a Purple Heart.

3. Bob Fenimore, 1947. One more time for Chicago, which selected the Oklahoma State standout first overall. Fenimore played in 10 games and then left football to sell life insurance.

4. Bo Jackson, 1986. Great player, except not for Tampa Bay, which chose "Bo Knows" at the top of the draft—not knowing Bo would go play major league baseball.

5. George Rogers, 1981. Not that he was a flop, but the Saints took him first overall and passed on Lawrence Taylor.

Five Best WR Picks

1. Raymond Berry, 1954. The best hands and best routes of his era marked Berry, who went from 20th-rounder to John Unitas's favorite target with Baltimore Colts and to the Hall of Fame.

2. Jerry Rice, 1985. Merely the most accomplished receiver in history, Rice's separation speed and pedigree coming out of Mississippi Valley State were questioned. He slipped to 16th overall, the 49ers gobbled him up, and he dominated defensive backs for nearly two decades.

3. Tom Fears, 1948. The Rams lived in Cleveland then, and they found Fears 103rd overall. He put fear in defenders for nine seasons on his way to the Hall of Fame.

4. Steve Largent, 1976. Houston chose the Tulsa product 117th overall. Then he was traded to expansion Seattle, taking his alleged plodding style with him. Largent became the Seahawks' greatest player and a Hall of Famer.

5. Wayne Millner, 1936. A rare standout pass catcher in a time when running the ball dominated, Millner was taken 65th overall by the Redskins in the first draft. He also played defense and helped win the '37 title. Another Hall of Famer who fell through the cracks.

Five Worst WR Picks

1. Charles Rogers, 2003. The poster child for failed pro careers at the position, Rogers went second in '03 to Detroit. He made more news with legal issues than anything he did with a football and spent only 15 games with the Lions.
2. Troy Williamson, 2005. Injuries ruined this dynamic speedster's pro career. He lasted five years after going seventh overall to Minnesota, but it was a wasted pick.
3. Mike Williams, 2005. Size and big-play skills made Williams an enchanting prospect. Then he couldn't learn routes or hold the ball in the pros, making the Lions' choice, 10th overall, a bust.
4. Matt Jones, 2005. Finishing off the horrid hat trick for '05, Jones impressed in predraft workouts but then never shone on the field. Selected 21st, he did better than Williamson and Williams, at least, in his four seasons.
5. R. Jay Soward, 2000. Soward's production at Southern Cal wowed the Jaguars, who used the 29th overall spot for him. He spent one season with Jacksonville and was gone, plagued by serious off-field issues.

Five Best Tight End Picks

1. Shannon Sharpe, 1990. From tiny Savannah State, Sharpe was an afterthought for Denver at 192nd overall. Yet he retired as the leading receiver at tight end and won three Super Bowls.

2. Charlie Sanders, 1968. Speed, endurance, and versatility—Sanders had all of that. Chosen 74th by the Lions, he solidifed the position in Detroit for a decade and made three All-Pro squads before entering the Hall of Fame.

3. John Mackey, 1963. The prototype of the modern tight end. Before Mackey, the 19th overall selection by the Baltimore Colts, TEs were blockers first and pretty much second. He showed he could get open downfield and get into the end zone.

4. Jackie Smith, 1963. A standout for 16 pro seasons, the first 15 with the Cardinals, Smith went from the 129th spot in the draft to the Pro Bowl and then to the Hall of Fame.

5. Dave Casper, 1974. Perhaps known best for his part in the "Holy Roller" play that changed NFL rules on advancing fumbles, Casper was a superb all-around tight end selected 45th overall.

Five Worst Tight End Picks

1. Tom Hutchinson, 1963. Cleveland grabbed him ninth overall out of Kentucky and got all of 19 catches and two TDs in three years. He spent one more season with Atlanta.

2. J. V. Cain, 1974. The Cardinals envisioned him as a do-everything tight end who would open up their offense. Instead, Cain, chosen with the seventh pick, never made more than 26 catches in his four pro seasons.

3. Ken McAfee, 1978. The son of a former NFL player and an All-American at Notre Dame, McAfee was projected as a surefire force when chosen seventh overall. He played decently in two NFL seasons with San Francisco and then retired because he felt the team didn't sup-

port his pursuit of a medical career. He became an oral surgeon.

4. Mike Cobb, 1977. Cobb spent all of one season with Cincinnati, which selected him 22nd overall. He hooked on with Chicago and lasted four more years but never with any impact—and with no TDs for his career.

5. Derek Brown, 1992. The Giants were looking for the next Mark Bavaro. Instead, they got an overmatched TE with the 14th overall pick and he caught only 11 balls for them in three seasons.

Five Best Offensive Tackle Picks

1. Lou Creekmur, 1948. Philadelphia stayed awake long enough in the grab bag to take the versatile two-way lineman from William and Mary at 243rd. Old-timers consider him among the best blockers in NFL annals.

2. Roosevelt Brown, 1953. The Giants went even deeper in this draft to find Brown, 321st overall. He anchored New York's line for 13 seasons and was the first player from Morgan State to make the Hall of Fame.

3. Art Shell, 1968. Shell's physicality embodied the style and power of the Raiders. Selected 80th out of Maryland-Eastern Shore, he made eight Pro Bowls and the Hall of Fame.

4. Jackie Slater, 1976. The 86th overall selection played 20 seasons for the Rams, made seven Pro Bowls, and then made the Hall of Fame. A superb technician, he never won a championship; at times he was the best player on the team.

5. Larry Allen, 1994. Sonoma State is hardly a college football factory. The Cowboys found Allen there, took him 46th overall, and he became a Hall of Fame blocker as a tackle and guard, among the strongest players in the game.

Five Worst Offensive Tackle Picks

1. Tony Mandarich, 1989. Don't need to know much more than he was surrounded by No. 1 pick Troy Aikman, No. 3 Barry Sanders, No. 4 Derrick Thomas, and No. 5 Deion Sanders. Green Bay thought he would anchor its line for years. Instead, he sank, plagued by steroids.
2. Bernard Williams, 1994. Drug use ruined Williams's career after being chosen 14th by Philadelphia. His rookie year was solid, but he never played again in the NFL after failing a drug test and not completing a treatment program.
3. Kevin Allen, 1985. Taken ninth overall by Philadelphia, Allen failed a drug test in his second season; he was arrested after that for sexual assault and banned from the NFL.
4. Andre Johnson, 1996. The 30th overall pick in 1996 by Washington, Johnson never got into a game as a rookie and was cut in 1997.
5. Chris McIntosh, 2000. Seattle got two mediocre seasons out of the 22nd overall pick. McIntosh was supposed to balance the offensive line on the other side of star left tackle Walter Jones, but a pinched nerve in his second season led to his being released in 2003.

Five Best Offensive Guard Picks

1. Gene Hickerson, 1957. Cleveland needed a road grader to lead the way for Jim Brown's devastating runs. The Browns found Hickerson in the seventh round. He blocked for Brown from Cleveland all the way to nearby Canton and the Hall of Fame.
2. Russ Grimm, 1981. The Hogs were considered among the most balanced offensive lines in NFL history, but

Grimm was the true standout. A real bargain at 69th, he helped the Redskins win three Super Bowls.

3. Dan Fortmann, 1936. Drafted by the Bears in the ninth round of the first selection process, Fortmann played some defense too. Fortmann was the youngest starter in the NFL at age 20, played eight seasons, and was an all-star in every one of them.

4. Jerry Kramer, 1958. The Packers could never have run to daylight without the 39th overall choice. Best known for his block to help win the Ice Bowl over Dallas, Kramer was an All-Pro in 5 of his 11 seasons.

5. Will Shields, 1993. Kansas City has always been adept at finding blockers in the draft. With the 74th spot, the Chiefs found this gem at Nebraska, and Shields made 12 straight Pro Bowls.

Five Worst Offensive Guard Picks

1. Rufus Guthrie, 1963. The 10th overall pick by the AFL's Chargers and by the NFL's Rams, the Georgia Tech product went to San Diego. He broke his ankle on the opening play of his first preseason game and never played in the pros.

2. Rod Walters, 1976. One of those Big Ten power guards the NFL loved in those days, Walters came out of Iowa as the 14th overall selection. He started seven games with the Chiefs in four years.

3. John Hicks, 1974. New York envisioned the dynamic Ohio State player as a cornerstone for its line. What the Giants found Hicks excelled at was holding. He lasted through four poor seasons.

4. Kurt Schumacher, 1975. The awful Saints were always in need of a talent boost. Schumacher came 12th overall

from Ohio State—yep, another Big Ten flop. He was tried at guard and tackle, started just 17 games in four seasons.

5. Steve Schindler, 1977. Schindler picked a good year to join the Broncos, who were Super Bowl bound. The only problem was the Boston College guard wasn't worth the 18th overall pick. He had four starts in two seasons.

Five Best Center Picks

1. Jim Otto, 1960. Deep into the AFL's first draft, Oakland went for this Miami center. Otto epitomized the battling nature of the Raiders, was the league's best center, and became a Hall of Famer.

2. Jim Ringo, 1953. Perhaps the second best at the position to Otto in pro football history, Ringo didn't go until 79th. He started in Green Bay for 11 seasons and in Philadelphia for 4 before making Hall of Fame.

3. Mike Webster, 1974. The man in the middle for the championship Steelers teams, he was a main cog in Pittsburgh's running game and then a key protector when the passing game developed. Selected 125th overall, he is also in the Hall of Fame.

4. Dermontti Dawson, 1988. The successor to Webster—as a Steeler and then in the Canton shrine—Dawson went 44th overall out of Kentucky. He started every game for 10 straight seasons.

5. Dwight Stephenson, 1980. Like Dawson, Stephenson brought tremendous athletic ability to the position, something unheard of in earlier days. A steal at No. 48 out of Alabama, he made four All-Pro teams in eight seasons. And yes, he's in the Hall of Fame too.

Five Worst Center Picks

1. Dave Behrman, 1963. Something of a bidding war took place when this Michigan State player was taken fourth in the AFL draft by Buffalo, 11th by Chicago in the NFL. The winner—uh, loser—was Buffalo, where Behrman managed to get in 28 games, no starts.
2. James Files, 1976. Taken 56th overall by Pittsburgh out of McNeese State, where he was a two-time Little All-American. But Files got hurt and never made it into an NFL game.
3. Robert Shaw, 1979. When you draft a center in the first round, something of a rarity, he'd better be a long-term answer. Shaw went to Dallas 27th overall and had six starts in three seasons.
4. Jesse James, 1995. Some might say he stole whatever money he got from the Rams, who grabbed him with the 62nd pick. He started two games in two seasons and then the posse chased him out of town.
5. Michael Cheever, 1996. Taken in Jacksonville's second year of life, Cheever went 60th overall and was supposed to be the Jags' snapper for years. He lasted two years, with six starts.

Five Best Defensive Ends

1. Deacon Jones, 1961. Perhaps the best pick in draft history at *any* position, Jones was a 14th-rounder by the LA Rams out of Mississippi Valley. He was an immediate starter and dominator on the Fearsome Foursome, and the term "sack" was invented for him. Jones played 14 seasons and then headed to Canton.

2. Willie Davis, 1956. One of the linchpins of Green Bay's strong defenses in its dynastic years, Davis came to the Packers in the 15th round out of Grambling. He never missed a game in his 12 pro seasons and was as strong in the fourth quarter as on the first snap.

3. Richard Dent, 1983. The MVP of the 1986 Super Bowl on perhaps the greatest one-season defense in NFL history, Dent was among the top pass rushers of his time. He had 137½ sacks in 15 seasons, including a league-best 17 in that championship year. His landing spot in the draft: 203rd.

4. Andy Robustelli, 1951. A leader for the great Giants teams of the 1950s and early '60s, Robustelli was taken 228th overall by the Rams and was a star in LA for five years before being traded to New York for a first-rounder that became standout receiver Del Shofner. Robustelli was a six-time All-Pro who played in eight NFL title games.

5. Elvin Bethea, 1968. One of the great pass rushers to come out of the AFL and perform even better in the NFL after the merger, Bethea was selected 77th by the Oilers. He made the Pro Bowl in half of his 16 seasons with Houston and was unblockable one on one.

Five Worst Defensive Ends

1. Jamal Reynolds, 2001. If not for Tony Mandarich, this would be the worst choice in Packers history. Drafted 10th overall, Reynolds played in 18 games over three seasons. Even worse, to get the spot for him, Green Bay dealt QB Matt Hasselbeck and a pick that became star guard Steve Hutchinson.

2. Kenneth Sims, 1982. A top overall pick by the Patriots, and he hung around for eight years. But he barely contributed in those seasons (all of 16 sacks) and was plagued by injuries.

3. Dimitrius Underwood, 1999. Taken 29th overall by Minnesota, Underwood had a mental meltdown and managed to play only 20 games in the NFL.

4. Steve Emtman, 1992. Bad knees limited Emtman's production for three teams over six years, with only one full season (1995 with Miami). Not so bad, you say? Well, the Colts made him the top overall pick in '92.

5. Eric Curry, 1993. Tampa Bay envisioned the second coming of Lee Roy Selmon when it took Curry sixth overall. After a strong rookie year, Curry's career spiraled and he never found a regular role with the Bucs.

Five Best Defensive Tackles

1. John Randle, 1990. OK, he wasn't drafted—shame on the NFL teams who felt he was too small and came from too tiny a school, Texas A&M–Kingsville. Randle became the top pass rusher from DT of his era, and a terrific all-around player with Hall of Fame credentials.

2. Henry Jordan, 1957. The Browns apparently had no idea what Jordan was capable of when they took him in the fifth round. He played two seasons in Cleveland, went to Green Bay, and became a five-time All-Pro and Hall of Famer.

3. Art Donovan, 1947. Ditto for the Giants, who used the 204th pick on Donovan, who didn't get to the NFL until 1950, when he was 26. And that was with the Colts, the

team the colorful Donovan won two NFL championships
with in his 10 seasons in Baltimore.

4. Arnie Weinmeister, 1945. As the war was ending, Weinmeister was selected 166th by the Boston franchise. He
   showed up in 1948 with the New York Yankees—yes,
   they were a football team—for two seasons and then
   played four years with the Giants. Despite such a short
   career, he made the Hall of Fame.

5. Joe Klecko, 1977. The only defensive player to make
   the Pro Bowl at three positions—tackle, end, and nose
   tackle—Klecko was Mr. Do It All for the Jets after going
   144th in the 1977 draft. Injuries shortened his career, but
   what a bargain he was for New York.

Five Worst Defensive Tackles

1. Steve Niehaus, 1976. Seattle's consolation prize for its first
   draft was this Notre Dame player, taken just behind Lee
   Roy Selmon going to Tampa. Selmon headed toward the
   Hall of Fame, Niehaus to Minnesota for one season after
   three mediocre years with the Seahawks.

2. Johnathan Sullivan, 2003. In what seemed a never-ending
   search for defensive talent up front, the Saints used the
   sixth spot on the Georgia tackle. He lasted three so-so
   seasons in the Big Easy.

3. Ted Gregory, 1988. The Saints didn't get it right 15 years
   earlier, either. After Denver selected Gregory 26th overall,
   the Broncos realized Gregory's knees were too damaged
   for the pros. But New Orleans wasn't so perceptive, it
   traded for him, and Gregory got into three games in his
   only season.

4. Ken Novak, 1976. A little further down from Niehaus in this draft, at No. 20, the Colts saw plenty of value in this Purdue DT. He never paid back their faith, appearing in 23 games with two starts before departing.

5. Justin Harrell, 2007. Green Bay had plenty of offense in the 2000s. It desperately needed an impact defender with some bulk. So Harrell was taken 16th overall—and managed only 14 starts in three seasons, with no impact. Injuries slowed him.

Five Best Linebackers

1. Joe Schmidt, 1953. Imagine getting the greatest defensive player in team history with the 85th pick in a draft. Detroit did so with Schmidt, out of Pitt, and he was a 13-season superstar, one of the game's most dominant linebackers.

2. Nick Buoniconti, 1962. Longevity was Buoniconti's, uh, long suit. He played fourteen seasons, the first seven with the Patriots, who selected him 102nd. For the other seven, he was the foundation of Miami's defense that won two Super Bowls.

3. Bobby Bell, 1963. If he wasn't the best linebacker the AFL had, Bell sure was close. Taken in the seventh round, he never missed a game in 12 seasons, was a force everywhere on the field, and made the Hall of Fame.

4. Ray Nitschke, 1958. Green Bay's answer to Chicago legend Dick Butkus at middle linebacker was Nitschke, whom the Packers grabbed in the third round in '58. Nitschke played hard, played hurt, and was the heart of Vince Lombardi's defense.

5. Harry Carson, 1976. Carson toiled with a losing franchise for the first half of his 13-year career with the Giants, who got him in the fourth round. He then became a mentor to New York's outstanding corps of linebackers and helped the Giants to their first Super Bowl win.

Five Worst Linebackers

1. Tom Cousineau, 1979. Imagine selecting an Ohio State LB with the top overall pick and then seeing him sign with the CFL. Yep, the Canadian Football League. Buffalo managed to do that, and even though Cousineau eventually played in the NFL, the choice was a total bust for the Bills.
2. Huey Richardson, 1991. The Steelers know their linebackers—do the names Ham and Lambert ring a bell? They struck out on this one, though; the 15th overall pick made it into just five games in Pittsburgh.
3. Billy Cannon Jr., 1984. Dallas loved the athleticism and local flavor that the son of a Heisman Trophy winner brought to Big D. Unfortunately, the 25th selection badly injured his neck and played only eight games.
4. Mike Junkin, 1989. No. 5 overall picks make sense from Duke—in basketball. Junkin started all of seven games in three seasons and had no impact. Despite being called a "mad dog in a meat market," by Cleveland scout Dom Anile, the scout thought he was a second-round talent.
5. Trev Alberts, 1994. Seven starts in three seasons for the fifth overall pick? Ugh! Alberts was best known for being the centerpiece of a feud between Colts GM Bill Tobin and draft expert Mel Kiper Jr.

Five Best Cornerbacks

1. Mel Blount, 1970. The prototype of the modern cornerback, Blount came to Pittsburgh as the 53rd overall selection. He was perfect for the Steel Curtain with his speed, versatility, and physicality, and wound up in the Hall of Fame.
2. Dick LeBeau, 1959. Many think LeBeau is enshrined in Canton because of his work as the Steelers' defensive coordinator. But he was voted into the hall thanks to his brilliant performances as a cornerback for 14 seasons with Detroit. But it was Cleveland that grabbed him 58th and then cut him. Nice move, Browns.
3. Lem Barney, 1967. Detroit found one of the originators of the term shutdown cornerback with the 34th pick. Barney rewarded the Lions with 56 career interceptions, exceptional work as a kick returner, and seven Pro Bowl appearances.
4. Ken Riley, 1969. Five spots into the sixth round, Cincinnati went for Riley, out of Florida A&M, a school known best for its marching band. Riley marched right onto the Bengals and stayed with them for 15 superb seasons, retiring with 65 picks.
5. Aeneas Williams, 1991. The versatile Williams was selected 59th overall by Arizona, made eight Pro Bowls (six with the Cardinals, two with the Rams), and also played some safety. He was physical, fast, and smart, and is a Hall of Famer.

Five Worst Cornerbacks

1. Bruce Pickens, 1991. Right from the outset Pickens's career was in trouble. He held out as a rookie and never

really caught up. After going third overall to Atlanta, Pickens wound up with four teams in four seasons, doing little with all of them.

2. Mike Rumph, 2002. Considering how strong San Francisco's secondary has been since the early 1980s, it's stunning the Niners missed so badly on Rumph at No. 27. He managed to stay in the league for five seasons, but Rumph was a liability throughout that time.

3. Rashard Anderson, 2000. The first of an Anderson hat trick, Rashard went to Carolina at No. 23. He flopped in his two seasons, unable to make the leap from Jackson State to the pros.

4. Billy Anderson, 1953. Chicago spent the sixth overall pick on the Compton Community College (California) two-way player, planning to make him into a cornerback. Instead, Anderson, one of the team's first African Americans, spent his rookie season primarily on offense and special teams. He only played 19 games for Chicago.

5. William Anderson, 1971. This Anderson could play safety and cornerback and was a standout at Ohio State. That sold the Niners, who used the 23rd pick on him—only to see him last just his rookie season in San Francisco. He also played two games for Buffalo.

Five Best Safeties

1. Ken Houston, 1967. A star for Houston, which chose him in the ninth round and then for Washington—he brought the Oilers five players in 1973—Houston was a premier playmaker. He played in 10 Pro Bowls on his way to the Hall of Fame.

2. Larry Wilson, 1960. Among the most versatile and rugged safeties in league history, Wilson had the misfortune to play for some mediocre teams in St. Louis. Chosen 74th, he was the face of the Cardinals franchise, made eight Pro Bowls, and played hurt. He intercepted one pass while wearing casts on both hands.

3. Jack Christiansen, 1951. He played for three championship teams with the Lions and made five Pro Bowls after going 69th overall. Christiansen was also a breakaway threat as a punt returner and made the Hall of Fame in 1970.

4. Yale Lary, 1952. Also an outstanding punter and kick returner, Lary went in the third round to the Lions and was a stalwart as they won three titles. Lary picked off 50 passes and made nine Pro Bowls despite serving in the army during the 1954 and 1955 seasons.

5. Paul Krause, 1964. One of the great ball-hawking safeties in NFL history, Krause went in the second round to Washington, played four seasons there, making two Pro Bowls. He then went to Minnesota for a dozen seasons, making another six Pro Bowls and the Hall of Fame.

Five Worst Safeties

1. Don Rogers, 1984. The 18th selection, by Cleveland, broke into the NFL nicely and looked like a real comer through two seasons. Then Rogers died of a heart attack in '86, triggered by cocaine use.

2. James "Yazoo" Smith, 1968. The 12th overall pick out of Oregon had little impact as a rookie and then hurt his neck and couldn't continue his career. He soon after sued the NFL, saying the draft was unconstitutional.

3. George Donnelly, 1965. The 13th pick in this draft spent three mediocre years with the 49ers. Maybe the Broncos, who took him in the fourth round, knew something the Niners didn't.

4. Russell Carter, 1984. Although he was drafted as a cornerback, the Jets discovered he couldn't cover receivers on the outside. Or much of anywhere else. He lasted six unmemorable seasons, the final two as a safety with the Raiders.

5. Patrick Bates, 1993. Remember all those sensational Raiders defensive backs who hit a ton and could cover like a blanket? Not Bates, the 12th overall pick, who lasted a so-so three seasons, one with Atlanta.

The setting of the 2014 NFL draft in Radio City Music Hall. With a remarkable cache of prospects, the 2014 draft drew an unprecedented number of viewers. Jamie Herrmann/AP Images.

Jadeveon Clowney—still a little teary-eyed as Houston's first pick. AP Photo/ Gregory Payan.

Johnny Manziel, the so-called Johnny Football. First freshman to win the Heisman Trophy and the 22nd overall pick that landed him in the Dawg Pound. Photo courtesy of Erik Drost.

Michael Sam—a last-minute pick for the Rams—asked only to be judged by his on-field credentials rather than the media circus surrounding his sexual identity. Here, he carries a piece of the rock "M" at Memorial Stadium after his final Mizzou home game. Photo courtesy of Mark Schierbecker.

President Truman receiving his annual pass to National Football League games from Bert Bell, commissioner of the National Football League and inventor of the draft (center), and George Marshall, owner of the Washington Redskins (right). Photo by Abbie Rowe, National Archives and Records Administration, Office of Presidential Libraries, Harry S. Truman Library.

Jay "The Flying Dutchman" Berwanger, winner of the first Heisman Trophy and first overall draft pick in 1936. AP Photo.

Tom Brady—the Pats' best pick—who went from being the 199th selection to Super Bowl champion in two seasons. Photo courtesy of Keith Allison.

Peyton Manning was the Colts' best pick until they released him as a free agent. Now he's the Broncos' superstar QB. Photo courtesy of Ian Ransley.

ESPN gurus: Mel Kiper Jr., Jon Gruden, and Chris "Boomer" Berman. Photo courtesy of Marianne O'Leary.

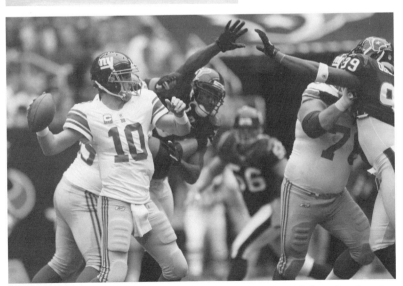

ROUND # ___1___ SAN DIEGO

CHOICE FROM: _____

NAME: _Manning_ _Eli_
      (Last)   (First)

POSITION: _QB_____

SCHOOL: _Mississipi_____

OVERALL # ___1_____

CHARGERS

The Chargers' draft card for Eli Manning in 2004. What the Chargers actually got was a very unhappy first overall pick. Photo courtesy of Matt McGee.

Eli Manning with the Giants. He (and dad Archie) was much happier after they forced his trade just an hour after being drafted by the Chargers. Photo Courtesy of AJ Guel.

John Elway, the number one overall pick for the (then) Baltimore Colts in the 1983 draft, got his way by threatening to sign with the Yankees instead. U.S. Air Force photo by Tech. Sgt. Marc Barnes.

8

WATCH THIS!

TV and the Digital Age

Pete Rozelle was stumped. The man considered the greatest commissioner in U.S. sports history had been approached by Chet Simmons, who was running this new cable TV entity called ESPN. Simmons had this wild idea: his network would televise the NFL draft.

"We had a need for programming back in 1980 and '81 as a start-up business," says John Wildhack, now ESPN's executive VP. "Any programming we could attach NFL to it was of particular interest to us. Chet pitched Pete: 'Let us televise your draft,' which at that time was held on a Tuesday and Wednesday in a ballroom at the [New York] Sheraton. Pete thought Chet was out of his mind, but said, 'Let's try it.'"

So try it they did—and the draft has gone from a cute football gathering to perhaps the third-most popular NFL event behind the Super Bowl and opening weekend of the season.

Don't underestimate the role ESPN (and, since 2006, NFL Network, too) has played in the ascension of the draft. The road to ratings that beat NBA and NHL playoff games in prime time has not been as smooth as a Montana to Rice TD pass, though.

ESPN had to scramble just to get ready for its first draft broadcast, which would take place on Tuesday, April 29, 1980.

"Chet Simmons called me to his office, and I had just started working there," says Bill Fitts, the original producer of the network's draft coverage.

> He tells me he wants to do the draft. This is in February for an April draft.
>
> I asked Chet, "Have you been there? There's no one there, except maybe friends of the owners, at the team tables. Not even a name assistant coach."
>
> Chet just looked back at me and said, "It is the NFL."
>
> I said I didn't know if we could make a TV show out of this. Chet's answer was, "That is why I hired you, and go do it."

Fitts had a solid NFL background, having handled games for NBC and CBS. He worked the first Super Bowl for CBS—the game was televised by that network, which owned NFL rights—and by NBC, which had the AFL. He had spent 18 years doing NFL games, which meant he had plenty of contacts within the league, a strong working knowledge of pro football, and, most important, the work ethic and resourcefulness to pull off the first-ever telecast of the draft.

He also knew he wouldn't have an unlimited budget at his fingertips.

"I would say at the beginning it was like with our golf coverage—we started covering one hole," he says, laughing. "Look what it went to."

Fitts's cohort for that initial draft broadcast was Frank Ross, who was writing for *Pro Football Weekly*. They combined to predict who they thought might go early in the draft and had remarkable accuracy. Fitts believes they wound up getting all but one player right in the first two rounds.

He recognized, though, that with so little going on visually, the telecast needed much more than talking heads jabbering their way through the selections.

So they asked the schools to send footage and sat for hours, edited the reels down into smaller packages, and loaded up on the stats.

The original plan was to be on the air for 12 hours, with the show beginning at 7:00 a.m. because the draft began in the morning back then. But Simmons also told Fitts if he thought it was wise to sign off early, it would be OK.

"But we had plenty of things to talk about," Fitts says. "And you know, we did not have Mel Kiper that year to talk about the players."

They did have a solid broadcasting crew that included one of ESPN's mainstays to this day, host Bob Ley. He was in the Bristol, Connecticut, studio with Upton Bell, the son of former NFL Commissioner Bert Bell; Howard Balzer of *Sporting News*; and Vince Papale, the former Eagle whose story became a movie, *Invincible*.

On hand in New York were former NFL team executive Joe Thomas and reporters George Grande, Spencer Ross, Bob Halloran, and Linda Sutter.

Balzer had the most journalistic chops when it came to the draft. In fact, his mock drafts were what got him hired by ESPN in the first place. He says,

> I was at *Sporting News* then, and we had done mock drafts for several years, but really, it wasn't a huge event.
>
> There was a certain amount of interest, but we might have been one of the first publications to do mock drafts.
>
> I know that [sportswriter] Frank Cooney had been doing the mock drafts, too. And the way it all developed, I got a call from a producer [at ESPN] maybe three or four weeks, at best, before the draft. The producer asks me—I think they were flying by the seat of their pants—"Can we use your mock draft in *Sporting News* on our broadcast?"
>
> I said, "Yeah, I am sure I can get permission, but you know how drafts go, after three picks it could go to crap. The top guys we had won't be picked, or others are gone we didn't have."

Balzer, who had been doing local radio shows in St. Louis, then said,

> If you want to get me on the phone, and we can do it, I can tell you, "Here is who we think will be the pick, or give analysis, or ask why did they do that, or say here is what is coming up next."
>
> He said it was not a bad thought, said he would throw it around.
>
> Then he calls me back and asks, "How would you like to come to Bristol to come on the show?"

Balzer knew his assignment: be prepared. Know who the players are.

As for highlights of the players, well, ESPN had not yet begun televising college football. In fact, few TV outlets were showing games because of NCAA rules that Gil Brandt, the former personnel director of the Dallas Cowboys and later the NFL's draft consultant, called "archaic."

So one of the staples of draft coverage over the last two decades was not a part of ESPN's earliest work.

Brandt recalls,

> They had all these crazy rules back in the '60s and '70s. A team could be on once a year or whatever. One or two TV games on a Saturday nationally.
>
> Now, Ohio State is on nine times a year. There's all the games on in one day: you can get 50 on TV on Saturdays. ESPN has games on from noon past midnight. All the cable channels, the Big Ten Network, and the others have games.
>
> It has taken the interest way up to another level for fans. They get to know all of those players in college, or at least they remember seeing them on TV, remember the names. I think people don't know and understand what a 3-technique is or understand play calling, but they do think they can be general managers, and they say, "Hey, why didn't this guy get drafted? I watched him play on TV and he is really good."

But for that first draft telecast, not so.

ESPN set up a remote at a restaurant, which Fitts said didn't work out too well, but it gave the proceedings a change of pace. The idea behind the remote was to find out how the fans thought it was going for the Giants. But with the fans somewhat subdued, there wasn't tremendous value in that approach in 1980.

Fitts liked that ESPN could inject some of the atmosphere on-site into the broadcast, that it could use a variety of talent in a different setting, not just sitting in the studio in Bristol. The last thing he wanted viewers to see and hear was what the same hosts and analysts were thinking, pick after pick.

"I thought it was amazing that it went so well; I thought I would be totally bored, but I was not at all," Fitts says. "Things went smoothly."

"The worst," Fitts adds, laughing, "was finding time to go to the john, 'cause I like to drink coffee."

ESPN might not have been off and running like Billy Sims, the first overall pick in 1980, had done at Oklahoma. But it was encouraged.

Many of the problems the network ran into emanated from a lack of experience. Like Sims would be that season, ESPN was a rookie at this game.

Among the challenges was trying to complete the story on a specific team's picks without falling too far behind the draft itself. That's easy enough in the first round when there was plenty of time (15 minutes) between picks. But as picks came closer together, it became harder to balance. And when viewers tune in, they want to know what their favorite team has done. Fitts had to figure out how to get to that information and still keep up with the (ongoing) picks.

"How long do you stay with a pick or a series of picks?" Fitts asks. "We found it was a matter of staying awake at the controls, adjusting to the changes. You go in with a plan, obviously—and then usually you throw it out the window after the third pick. All sports producing is reaction time. You learn that doing games or whatever else you are producing. The draft was no different."

Ah, but the draft was very different. It didn't have a true scoreboard, and the results—success and failure—might not be known for years.

What ESPN did know after that first broadcast was that Simmons's request of Rozelle was a wise one. The network just might have had something special on its hands.

Wildhack says,

> I think the draft has so many different elements to it: intrigue, rumor, innuendo, anticipation. In some ways it's the start of the next season. That's a combo of elements that makes the draft unique and obviously appeals to NFL fans, and to all football fans. For college football fans it is a huge day, too, with bragging rights: which school has more picks, which conference has more, who has higher picks. It's a confluence for both sets of fans.
>
> And it's the ultimate reality TV. You don't know who will get picked or where. You don't know who will be the winner, now or even for a few years. That provides mystery.

ESPN's challenge was simple in 1981 and thereafter: build on all those components. The NFL would go right along with that building, too, upgrading the venues in size, character, and cachet. Exploring different days and time slots. Bringing to the draft site players who were about to go from collegians to professionals. Even jazzing it all up like an awards show.

But first, after those significant initial steps in 1980, ESPN needed to stamp the draft telecasts in its own way. Give them some personality. Add to the on-camera expertise. Make the draft a big deal.

"As we had more money, we started to do things better," Fitts says. "We got remotes going from the teams' sites. We started doing stuff from NFL Films. We would find different things to do to keep up with things. There were more pieces to it, more people working on it, so it got more complex. But everything as the company grew got more complex."

Adds Wildhack, "You learn as you go, refine it, but I don't think there ever was a time we said, 'This didn't work whatsoever.' In the early days, we wanted to make sure we had highlights on every player. We thought that was pretty cool, and I think the fans and viewers did, too."

Still, something else was needed. Everyone involved in the telecasts early on recognized that ESPN had to enhance the experience for the viewer while also upgrading the presentation of information. In other words, make it fun but also make it educational.

Two people brought that combination to fruition: Chris Berman and Mel Kiper Jr.

An ESPN original, Berman was not yet "Boomer" to his colleagues and to the fans. He was a jack-of-all-trades broadcaster: an anchor on *SportsCenter*; a play-by-play man; an interviewer; an originator of nicknames, naturally; and even a setup man for some of his partners.

By adding Berman to the draft telecast, Fitts unwittingly began the upward spiral in Berman's career that led to everything from Berman's rapid-fire descriptions of highlights to "The Swami." In many ways, Berman became the headline voice at the network. And in many ways, the draft became his vehicle. Berman says,

> Here is what I always knew and I realized real quickly as a broadcaster—that the season ended on Feb. 1 or whatever the day was of the Super Bowl, and the draft was an oasis in the desert. In April we get to talk about football? Wow, let's go!
>
> It's a congregation of football fans drinking in that oasis, and then we all disappear until July and training camps.
>
> Remember that there was not the scene we have now in February and March, with the combine and the free agency period. We

realized this was not just a passing thing; this draft popularity was going to be even bigger. Football was king already, and everyone was realizing it.

By 1983, Berman believed the draft was ready to explode into a must-see event and that ESPN needed to seize the opportunity to make it a signature telecast on the network. Wildhack says that year was an early watershed moment for the telecasts:

> It was not lightning in a bottle immediately, but it didn't take too long before we understood how it was resonating.
>
> One major factor: the '83 draft, when [John] Elway was No. 1 overall, and declared he would not play with the Colts and would sign with the Yankees. That was a massive news story, not just a draft story.
>
> The QB class that year catapulted the draft to new heights, too. Elway, [Jim] Kelly, [Dan] Marino at the end; six quarterbacks in the first round.

Most everybody tends to know about the quarterbacks, though, whether it is college or the pros. It is, by far, the most publicized position in pro sports.

For the football-savvy Berman, researching the quarterbacks was the simple stuff. He had to go deeper, which meant not gearing up as the draft drew closer but diving in headfirst in the dead of winter. After all, he'd spent late July through the Super Bowl with the NFL, not the collegians, as his main focus.

Berman says,

> We are, of course, aware of what the teams had when the season ended. I am not starting from scratch, although I am new to it a bit because I have not been in on [the evaluations of college players]. You are learning the college players, if not from scratch, still learning them. Is that third tackle in the rankings as good as the other two who will go high, or is there a dropoff? That is new info to me, and to other people, and what we needed to get to the viewers.

You then kind of piece together what teams are telling you about the guys and how you think the flow will go. Your starting point is a lot farther back than for the league on a week-by-week basis, when you know the standings and how teams have been playing, who might be injured . . . I find it intriguing the way it unfolds.

Berman's legwork for the draft has been concentrated in a different area than his week-by-week research and interviewing during the season. He's far more involved with gathering information from general managers, scouts, and personnel directors, rather than from coaches. Every day during the NFL season—and even quite a bit in the preseason—Berman is getting down with coaches and players.

Not so much the case come February and March during the countdown to the draft.

"When you do the work for the last month the way I do it, it is really intense, especially the last three weeks," says Berman.

By the time those last three weeks arrive, Kiper's homework has pretty much been done. With the exception of juggling the order of picks in his mock draft, Kiper is in the waiting mode that, coincidentally, the college players are in.

Of course, three decades ago, Kiper was in a different sort of waiting mode—waiting to be discovered.

Exceptional journalist that he is, Balzer already knew what Kiper could offer to ESPN's broadcasts. ESPN executives encouraged all of the "talent" involved in the broadcast to send ideas on how to improve coverage. When ESPN decided to display a huge draft board, Berman and Balzer anchored that portion of the coverage.

Balzer remembers,

They would go to us every now and then and we would discuss who was still on the board, who was gone. None of us knew who put together the board, whether it was one person or who at ESPN. No one was getting any credit.

I sent them a note: "You got Mel Kiper Jr., he does rankings, so if you have this board you should have him in front of the board, and he talks about the players who just went or who remain, and what the team did. He defends them or not."

"They thought it was such a great idea, and they brought Mel to New York for the draft," Balzer adds with a chuckle, "and I wasn't in New York anymore."

Kiper would eventually create a cottage industry as a draft guru (see chapter 11). But back then, he was trying to establish a foothold as a draft expert—in much the same way ESPN was seeking to create a reputation as a sports leader in broadcasting.

As he sat with Fred Gaudelli, then an assistant but who would become the draft's producer in 1990, Kiper knew that by the midway point of the second round in 1987, he would be done. The draft was still going on, yet Kiper was headed back to Baltimore. He was even home in time to watch some of the later picks.

But he soon realized it paid to stay in New York for the entire draft even if he wasn't on the air. Gaudelli did much of the same: two football fans examining the ins and outs of every team's selections.

In 1993, Gaudelli told Kiper that it paid to scope out every pick "to see how the second day differs from the first."

Kiper asked why, and Gaudelli told him, "Because next year, we will be televising every pick."

That news fit in Kiper's throwing lane the way one of Brett Favre's tight spirals would pierce a defense. He felt the TV audience was being deprived of reams of information—his info, of course—because the middle and, especially, the latter rounds had been ignored on the telecasts. Kiper says,

> It was exciting to be able to do it, and those are the kind of rounds
> I gear to the most, the fifth through seventh. They are never house-

hold names—outside of the rarity—and it is great to bring to light these players and what they can and can't do and how they fit into the team.

It's great to have the opportunity to talk about a kid from Alcorn State or Coastal Carolina or Eastern Washington or Stephen F. Austin. It's right in my wheelhouse, and I never had a chance to do it.

Kiper called Gaudelli a trailblazer and predicted doing the entire draft would be a breakthrough for ESPN. It also was a career-making step for Kiper.

He even had to prevent himself from being in awe working with Berman and Ley, the first two people he met at ESPN and two of his broadcasting mentors.

"Hey, Chris is the voice of the NFL, whether it's the draft or anything else he is doing," Kiper notes. "When we would see Bob with his blue index cards, that is when we knew it is draft time. I was 23 when I started and green as grass, no experience on TV whatsoever, and for Chris to be as welcoming and encouraging and helpful, and the same thing for Bob, it made everything work better."

Kiper's impact on ESPN's telecasts should not be minimized. Every player, whether it is Johnny Football or some Johnny-come-lately who can kick a football, gets personalized by Kiper on the telecasts.

That he now has a Jon Gruden or Steve Young to bounce his opinions off makes for exactly the kind of TV Berman claimed was necessary to grow the audience. And ensure it is a knowledgeable audience.

That it took a while for ESPN to realize the value of gavel-to-gavel coverage only makes it more rewarding for Kiper. He says,

> The perception has changed immeasurably from it being just the first round that people only cared about to them craving more and more, and televising it all. Hey, guess what, they watch.
>
> The draft has proved people wrong every time. Still into the early 2000s people were bashing the extensive coverage. But all the naysayers were looking like idiots.

People watch because it is a critical weekend in the NFL. What else are you getting in late April or early May? You want to hear who your team is picking, see who it is picking; you crave that. And at that point when we went to every pick, it was on a Tuesday.

Extending its coverage to include everything down to Mr. Irrelevant (the final choice of the seven rounds) was a master stroke. In many ways, it magnified Kiper's expertise.

Just ask Berman.

"With Mel, I can ask him anything, especially when we would get to the middle of the third round and on," Berman says. "Now we are at the point where I say, 'The Saints just drafted Joe Smith, a cornerback from McNeese State.' And Mel would then go for five minutes about Joe Smith of McNeese State."

While Berman remained the master of ceremonies on what increased from a relatively simple setting to a 32-ring circus, Kiper was ESPN's supreme juggler. He remains so today, with a schedule that would make a workout fiend shy away.

Kiper has regular stints on a variety of ESPN programs, on TV and radio. He also hosts a radio show, writes columns, and reports on the draft. He's a multimedia megastar.

But the three days of the draft are when his star shines brightest. Kiper has his critics, but even they admit his impact on the grab bag that is the draft has been massive.

Berman isn't so quick to credit ESPN as the key to the draft's rocketing popularity. But he does have an insightful outlook on the importance of TV in the equation.

I'm not sure it was what we did that made it spike.

I started being the host in the 1980s, by the '90s I realized that this is our convention—and we did it every year, not every four years [like the presidential conventions].

Our job is to inform and to make it entertaining. With picks every 15 minutes in the first round until recently, admittedly some of the action was a little slow. When the picks are happening fast, it was like the combo between a ballgame and a convention, all of a sudden there was a lot of action.

Balzer is more emphatic in his evaluation of ESPN's—and especially Kiper's—role in elevating the draft's profile.

"There's no doubt TV mushroomed it," Balzer says, "and when Mel went on ESPN, that certainly drove it even more and created this cottage industry of books and magazines and everything on the Internet. People love that stuff."

By 2006, NFL Network had grasped just how much the people loved it. The NFL-owned cable channel opted to join the fray, even if it meant going head-to-head against ESPN.

Viewers can judge for themselves who does the best job. But just the fact that no NFL games, except for the exhibitions when both teams have local TV deals in the preseason, get the double-broadcast treatment says plenty about the draft's appeal.

The networks coexist peacefully, although fans on hand at the proceedings always seem to heckle and scream at the ESPNers more than the NFL Network guys.

"A lot of us when we sit at the same meetings and tables [with the league], it is the equivalent to an election job," says Charlie Yook, coordinating producer of the NFL Network's draft coverage. "They do a great job at ESPN and we do a great job, I feel, to portray the drama and the must-see TV, to borrow a phrase from NBC."

Like ESPN, NFL Network has hundreds of people involved in the telecasts, with many not even on-site. In many ways, it is the network's best chance to attract viewers, especially with the league having reduced the live Thursday-night game package on NFL Network to half a season; CBS bought the other half in 2014.

"The draft is in the perfect spot, whether in the last week in April or early in May," Yook says. "The NBA and NHL playoffs are starting, but people start to realize they really miss football and it offers a connection to their teams."

That connection is often laced with drama, and nowhere is that more apparent than in the green room—the place the collegians hang out until they are chosen. The backstage room is usually packed at the outset and for much of the first round, with players; their families, friends, and agents; league workers; and TV personnel. It's where those players find out they have been selected.

It's also where they sit and wait, and sometimes wait far longer than projected, to hear their names called.

Many viewers find the action in the green room more interesting than the actual selections.

According to Yook,

> It's what the fans want to see, yes, it's a fair point. If you are a fan of a team or a kid or the college he went to, you wonder where he will go and there is a lot of drama. And if he starts to slip. . . .
>
> Johnny Manziel is the primary name when you look at that recently, but of course there have been many others. With a player like that, a star on the football field and off the field, people always are following him. He is here or he is there, they want to know . . . he is the new-age star.

So having cameras in the green room brings an added layer of drama. It adds to that feel of it being an awards show.

"But we have to be sure it does not distract the viewer from what is truly going on," Yook adds.

One element that became very distracting occurred in the early 2000s when ESPN got wind of who had been picked before it was announced. When NFL Network joined the draft coverage in '06, it also fell into the trap of tipping viewers who would be next to walk across the stage and hug the commissioner.

In this age of stressing instantaneous fulfillment, decisions were made to televise live the players' reactions to being the next pick, even though the audience on-site had not yet been told who was chosen.

It made for bad theater. Yook explains,

> The league and its broadcast partners have agreed to not tip the pick, not show the player on the cellphone before getting selected. We all just decided it didn't help the broadcast; you ruined the TV part of it.
>
> I know it is very hard in this day and age with Twitter and everything else, and we can't control that. We have decided that we don't reveal that, though, especially those first two nights in prime time. No one wins in that situation and you are losing the drama of it.

That doesn't necessarily apply for the final four rounds because, as Yook notes, "the picks are flying, they get five minutes but some picks come one after the other, so you are not tipping really anything."

According to Yook, certain elements of the broadcasts are givens:

- Don't miss a pick. "That first night, you have only the 32 and we treat them all equally, and this is a special moment for those players, we can't forget that."
- Stress the meaning of the pick. "This could be potentially a life-changing moment for teams and fans, but definitely it is one for the player. So we need to make sure we cover those moments on the stage when they meet the commissioner, put on the hat, and hold up the jersey. Cover it respectfully and with due diligence."
- Don't get lost looking at the big picture the first two days. "The coverage is usually centered on the here and now those first two days, what is happening. We plan way ahead

with the elements we want so we can be reactionary to things like teams who move up and down."

- Find something different for the third day of the grab bag. "Day 3 is more a bigger picture look. Where does this person help? Where and when can they contribute? We look at all of the divisions, grading them. We're not analyzing pick by pick when we get to Day 3, and we realize we still have some bigger names who drop down and wind up in those rounds. Some quarterbacks fall. In [2014], we had Michael Sam."

- Emphasize the mystery. "What is driving everything is you just don't know who will turn into what kind of player. Remember, a seventh-rounder was Super Bowl MVP [Malcolm Smith in 2014]. We model our broadcast to make this like a new beginning, offering hope for the fans. Isn't that what the draft does?"

Surely. And that's why Mike Mayock is such a critical part of NFL Network's telecasts.

To say Mayock holds the Kiper role at NFL Network would be an unfair comparison. Each has his own original style, each is as busy as anyone in the broadcast business, and both have been essential to the growth of the audience in all avenues the draft touches.

Especially on TV.

"The interest on TV blows me away," Mayock admits. "Look at the ratings on both ESPN and NFL Network for the [2014] draft, and compare them to the NBA or NHL playoff games. The draft blows them away. PLAYOFF GAMES! I can't even begin to imagine that an event like the draft can overshadow a professional playoff game. Yet it does, and in a big way."

Why it does so goes well beyond sports, Mayock believes. He points to the overwhelming number of reality shows on the tube and calls the draft the ultimate of such programs.

"I know a ton of people who tune in to see the drama of Johnny Manziel sliding. And they are not NFL fans particularly," he says. "But the idea of a player sitting there with his family, in that green room, and the emotions as he doesn't get picked. I know a lot of people who would not watch a game but are hooked on the drama of the green room, and every 10 minutes there is another selection to add drama."

So when an Aaron Rodgers, Geno Smith, Tim Tebow, Brady Quinn, or Manziel see their stock fall—just to mention some quarterbacks since 2005—their angst becomes palpable. That, in turn, intrigues the viewers, sports fans or not.

"I totally recognize the drama of certain players like Tim Tebow and Manziel," Mayock says. "On TV, we want to support the national interest in these players. The football purist in me hates it because sometimes we forget there are other players, and it is the biggest night of their lives. But these are stories that need to be told and have drawn so much interest."

What doesn't particularly appeal to Mayock the football purist are the red carpets and green rooms, the feel that the selection process has turned into something of an awards show.

"I will always be a high school football coach's son, so the draft should be about the selections," he says. "But the pragmatic side of my brain understands the demand. I just sometimes think the purpose of the draft can get lost."

It surely helps on TV that there is a sense of competition between ESPN and NFL Network. No one seems to welcome that more than Kiper.

"I was the one who wanted Todd McShay to be on TV with me and on the draft," he says of an ESPN sidekick.

I wanted another opinion, a counter opinion if possible. Nothing we ever do is contrived. We talk about how we feel, but whatever it is, it is real.

NFL Network's broadcasts bring even more attention to the draft, and that's just what you want. I think it's great that Mike Mayock does such an outstanding job for NFL Network and there is even more interest in the draft because of that.

The more people watching or talking about the draft, the better that is for all of us.

How about the more people listening? ESPN has carried the draft live on radio since 1992, although it has never done every pick. That assignment, since 2004, has been left to SiriusXM NFL Radio.

The satellite radio company, which has a deal with the NFL that includes carrying every team radio broadcast live for regular-season games, has become as much a part of the electronic coverage of the draft as anyone. Even though, perhaps, it didn't feel all that welcome at the outset.

"At our first draft show, we were in a kind of corridor at a table with no skirts," Brandt recalls. "You had to find your way to us. Now, everyone is wanting to have a show at the draft and everyone wants to be on SiriusXM."

That first radio broadcast by Sirius's Channel 88 included Brandt, Phil Simms, Pat Kirwan, and Steve Cohen, who put together Sirius's sports network of channels a decade ago—well before the company merged with XM.

Brandt and Kirwan, a former NFL personnel director, have been involved in every one of the channel's draft broadcasts since. Others who have joined have included ex-players John Riggins, Shannon Sharpe, and Cris Carter—all Hall of Famers—as well as Tim Ryan, Jim Miller, Randy Cross, and Ross Tucker.

NFL insiders such as Bill Polian and Phil Savage have also played a role in draft coverage. The idea, as Kirwan says, is to give fans "every kind of opinion from every kind of viewpoint."

Adam Schein, who was only 26 when he was Cohen's first hire at NFL Radio, has moved elsewhere at SiriusXM. He still has a draft-day jones, though.

"I loved hosting the draft every year," says Schein, who anchored the coverage for eight years. "I never looked at it as competition: ESPN and NFL Network have it on TV, SiriusXM has it on radio. The buzz we would always get was incredible. The drama, the fun, the great guests, it was incredible radio."

Schein cites an interview with Rams draft choice Janoris Jenkins in 2012 after the North Alabama cornerback was chosen in the second round. Jenkins had several off-field incidents, and he transferred from Florida to the smaller school.

"When we asked Janoris Jenkins if he can be compared to Pac-Man Jones, his response was: 'I ain't never shot up no strip club.'"

Kirwan, an astute analyst regarding college talent, might watch more video of players than any scout, coach, or general manager. He brings all of that knowledge to the microphone; hey, it's not easy filling all those hours when there are no visuals to keep the folks at home alert and entertained.

"I meet all the draftables," Kirwan says of his preparation, "and use that as my draft interview for the pool of players. Often, I ask the guys who seem particularly eager if they want to come on the show. If they are as intelligent as I think they are, they see an opportunity. And then I say I will send their [audio] tapes around to the GMs."

Because so many GMs and personnel people throughout the league listen to SiriusXM NFL Radio, those draft prospects suddenly have another road to recognition through the airwaves.

Is the end of the spectacular rise in popularity of the draft within sight? Just the opposite, it seems.

"I can tell you there will be massive interest in it as the sport gets bigger and bigger," NFL Network's Yook says.

An event like this only gets bigger, especially when you get names like the Manziels and Tebows coming out of college.

My hope is that we continue to push the envelope as far as access goes. One of our biggest selling points is what we can be able to show as far as the "war rooms" where teams make their decisions, and draft parties. At some point, it would be great, if there are four or five days of the draft, an extended event, that when we get to the later rounds, the teams from their war rooms make the pick live and on TV.

Anything we can give to the viewer to see inside where they can't see is what we are interested in.

ESPN's Berman remembers "when cable wasn't all that well known and lots of people didn't have cable. And then all of a sudden, they can watch [the draft] and people are calling in sick to their jobs on Tuesdays."

"Who the hell thought that?"

9

FAN FRENZY

The word *fan* is short for fanatic, and nowhere in the world of pro football is NFL fans' fanaticism more on display than at the draft.

Dressed in team colors—meaning jerseys, sweatpants, hats, helmets, and most notably, often in face paint—they converge on the draft venue like red ants marching toward a carcass. Sometimes, they threaten as much danger as an army of ants, too: if their team makes an unpopular pick, watch out.

"Early on, it was usually New York fans," says Howard Balzer, who has written about and broadcast the draft for more than three decades. "It always seemed more Jets fans than Giants fans, and the Jets were always making bad picks in their minds. Now, you see more of the reactions of fans and more and different teams' fans, and you see those clips of them going nuts and it sticks in your mind."

But the folks televising the draft knew not to go overboard concentrating on the fans—at least during the early years of the telecasts in the 1980s.

"There was not much of a crowd the first year, and mostly Jets and Giants fans, so we didn't have the crowd support you have now, not even close," says Bill Fitts, who produced the first few ESPN telecasts, beginning in 1980. "Usually we'd have some Cleveland fans, I don't understand why, but they would be there.

Otherwise, sporadic fans. And you can't get too involved in that. A quick shot of their reaction is about it, negative or positive."

Fitts recognized that the approval of the fans can be just as emphatic as the vitriol, too.

Two examples stand out from recent years, after the site of the draft was moved from a comparatively cozy Manhattan ballroom to the theater attached to Madison Square Garden and then to Radio City Music Hall, which could cram in 4,000 spectators.

First, the big hit, and not one delivered by a Lawrence Taylor (1981, 2nd overall) or Ray Lewis (1996, 26th overall). And then the downer.

They came within minutes of each other.

In 1999, the Browns returned to Cleveland, a city whose gridiron heart had been ripped apart when team owner Art Modell moved the franchise to Baltimore after the 1995 season. But other NFL owners and commissioner Paul Tagliabue insisted the city would get an expansion team and acted quickly on that promise.

So now, in the spring of '99, football was alive on the shores of Lake Erie. They had a new stadium, with a spanking new team calling it home—and even a specific section of stands for the colorful Browns rooters, the Dawgs.

And it seemed as if the entire Dawg Pound was transplanted to the Theater at Madison Square Garden for the draft.

The Browns would step to the plate first. The entire direction of the new club could be determined by who was chosen and how he fared as a pro.

In the audience were such illustrious (at least in Cleveland) Brownies as Big Dawg; you surely remember the masked face and the number 98 jersey worn by John Thompson, who actually had his name legally changed to Big Dawg. He seemed to bring the entire kennel along with him from Ohio for the historic selection.

At least it sounded that way.

Long before the proceedings began, the barking had commenced. At times, it was in unison, sort of a Cleveland Clatter—one fan called it the "Ohio Hum." At other instances as the building filled up, it was almost as if the Browns fans were competing with each other to make the most outrageous sounds and invent some offbeat cheer.

One phrase nobody in Browns colors was uttering: "Get off the Couch."

Oh, no, they wanted their Couch, Kentucky quarterback Tim Couch. And they knew they were getting him.

Chris Palmer, who made his mark as an offensive guru and was getting his first shot at being a head coach, and general manager Dwight Clark, a former star receiver with San Francisco, would make the pick, advised by team president Carmen Policy, another refugee from the 49ers.

And even though they spoiled the suspense by agreeing to a contract with Couch hours before Tagliabue announced the pick, the Browns had sated the appetites of their rabid followers.

As Tagliabue stepped to the podium to anoint Couch as the top choice, the makeshift Dawg Pound in the balcony began chanting: "Here we go, Brownies, here we go." When Couch walked onstage, the sound mimicked what shook the old Cleveland Stadium when Jim Brown was doing his thing and the Browns were actually contenders.

Even the voice of Chris "Boomer" Berman, anchoring coverage for ESPN, couldn't compete with what the fans were producing.

Soon after, Couch posed for photographs with Browns owner Al Lerner. Policy bragged that Couch, who left Kentucky after his junior season, "displayed so much character and poise. He's such a solid human being."

The Dawg Pounders just kept on barking.

"The thinking was clear and the thinking made sense: the Browns have got to have a quarterback, and they took Couch and got their quarterback, darn it," says ESPN's Berman. "I remember part of the reaction from the crowd was that the pick solidified that they were back in the NFL. It was the fans saying, 'We are back and we picked a quarterback, and this is our Frank Ryan.'"

Alas, Couch would be yet another mistake by the lake. Not too far into that first season, with Couch struggling mightily and showing he was not ready for pro football—he never would be able to handle the NFL—the fan base turned on him. He cried during an interview when asked about those fans whose bark turned into biting ridicule.

Indeed, it sort of resembled the greeting Donovan McNabb received just minutes after Couch left the theater stage on draft day.

Philadelphia was up next in the pecking order, and new coach Andy Reid had a superb chance to make a ton of friends in the City of Brotherly Booing, uh, Loathing, uh, Love. All he had to do was have the Eagles submit their card with the name Ricky Williams on it.

Eagles fans, decked out in their midnight green from head to toe—some sporting silver kerchiefs to match their face paint—had been cheering "RICK–EE, RICK–EE" even before they found their seats. After Cleveland grabbed Couch, the field was clear for Philly to take the Heisman Trophy–winning running back from Texas, a college game-breaker with power and speed.

Surely Reid would come through.

As the Eagles contemplated their choice, the theater became Longhorns Central. More chants of "RICK–EE." Some foot stomping, too. If the Eagles took Williams, it seemed logical the place would be overwhelmed by "Hook 'em Horns" shouts and a rendition of "The Eyes of Texas Are Upon You."

Then Tagliabue announced, "With the second pick, the Philadelphia Eagles select Donovan McNabb, quarterback, Syracuse University."

Before Tagliabue had gotten past saying Donovan, the Philly Phanatics—no not the cute baseball mascot but the wild Eagles fans—released their venom.

Screams of "OH, NOOOO," "WHAT??" and "YOU'RE KIDDING" were about the only printable ones heard through the din.

As poor McNabb held an Eagles jersey and posed with Tagliabue onstage, the chants of "WE WANT RICK–EE" resumed, this time tinged with anger.

And when New Orleans coach Mike Ditka traded all of his picks in 1999 to move up to fifth to get Williams, the uproar resumed.

As one Eagles fan, sporting a tattoo of the team's mascot on his left bicep, said as he exited the arena after the opening round, "I give up on them. Ditka knows what he's doing, and he trades the whole draft for Ricky Williams. And look what we get."

It could have been worse for the Eagles' faithful, who would have been yet more enraged had the team gone with its other top-ranked player.

"We had one running back we thought was outstanding, Edgerrin James," Eagles owner Jeffrey Lurie said. "But it was a no-brainer to go with the franchise quarterback."

So the team didn't even consider Williams the top runner in the '99 crop. Andy Reid, in his first year as Eagles coach, was looking at another position, anyway.

Berman said,

> I knew what he thought of McNabb. But the mayor of Philadelphia had fueled the fire on Ricky Williams. Ricky's college career speaks

for itself, and the mayor wasn't alone in thinking Ricky was the best player in the draft.

There is a team and staff that had the courage of their convictions, the Eagles. And it was certainly not the first time Philly fans booed something.

Yet Reid and the Eagles turned out to be the only smart ones.

I think of Andy Reid, his first pick ever, he did one of the most unpopular things in the history of the draft. Eagles fans were saying, "This is what we are starting off with in the new regime in Philadelphia?"

But that is when you have done your homework and you know what you are doing and you get it right.

The Eagles, of course, were correct, and McNabb became one of the best players in team history. Yes, Williams was a good, albeit unpredictable and at times unreliable, pro. But on that spring day in 1999, he was the potential savior to Philly fans, and McNabb was an imposter.

Soon after, Cleveland and Philadelphia would learn the truth about Couch and McNabb. Maybe the fans even began to recognize that the draft game should not be a popularity contest.

Dawg outfits and midnight green paint notwithstanding.

10

THE UNDERWEAR OLYMPICS

I t was *Meet the Press*, football style.

The hard questions came flying at Johnny Manziel fast and furious at the 2014 NFL combine.

Why had he refused to participate in the quarterback drills? Was he receiving counseling for an alcoholic problem and anger management? Was he too short to play in the National Football League?

More than 300 media members attended the 15-minute news conference at Lucas Oil Stadium in Indianapolis, home of the Colts. Reporters were there to cover the annual weeklong event as hundreds of college football players performed physical and mental tests for NFL coaches, scouts, and general managers.

One of the main attractions at the combine was Manziel, an atypical quarterback with a flair for the dramatic.

In a typical year, more than 300 players show up at the combine—all by special invitation. Among the tests and evaluations: 40-yard dash, bench press, vertical jump, broad jump, 20- and 60-yard shuttle, cone drill, and position-specific drills. Not to forget team interviews, in 15-minute intervals, and various mental evaluations.

It's officially known as the NFL Scouting Combine. Whimsically, it's called the "Underwear Olympics" because the players work out in shorts and without shoulder pads.

Held in Indianapolis in February, a few weeks after the Super Bowl, the combine is a precursor to the NFL draft held about two months later. A good performance will improve a player's draft stock based on size, speed, strength, and dexterity. A poor performance might lower his position in that year's draft.

A top agent, Joe Linta, said,

> Unless you're inhibited by injury, you should do everything at the combine, all the drills. That's what I tell [the players] and most of the time they listen to me.
>
> An offensive lineman one time came to me and said that he didn't want to work on something at the combine, he wanted to wait for his pro day. I told him, "This will raise red flags." And then five O-line coaches approached me that night: "What is up with that kid?" It raised those red flags.

At the 2014 combine, the controversial Manziel was one of those who skipped the quarterback drills. He told the media he had wanted to participate, but his agent persuaded him to wait until his pro day to showcase his talents for all 32 teams. That would be a couple of weeks in the future when players from Texas A&M would work out in front of visiting NFL coaches and scouts on their home field. Linta continued,

> The most important thing is that the decision makers from the NFL teams come in and get to see you and spend time with you. The pro days can run the whole gamut. Guys who had a great college career and a great combine don't have to do much at a pro day.
>
> But the others, the ones who were not invited to the combine, the pro day is their Super Bowl. They have to be ready to go and show their stuff, because they probably will not get a second chance. So, yeah, the pressure is on.

That pressure builds right from the time a college player's eligibility expires, when it becomes agent time. After all-star games for many of the top prospects, agents set up programs at training facilities. Then comes the combine and pro day for their clients in a buildup to the draft.

"He's sent to a recommended training facility, places we have good success with, and the fun begins," said Linta, who usually represents 8 to 12 guys a draft and has had about 75 players drafted in 20 years. "Part and parcel is getting them transportation, food, supplements if they use them, a soup-to-nuts deal between us [as agents] and the player."

Everything is geared toward the combine when they are at these training facilities. It's rare that players get a one-on-one workout, but usually they are in groups, 10 to 15 players, and with a team of trainers.

"They'll do drills for a few hours in the morning, take a break, then chiropractic and massage and yoga and swimming and the like," Linta said.

In most days, they will actually have some football mixed in, lest they forget why they are there.

According to Linta,

> We might bring in a coach like Chris Palmer, which we did this year for [LSU quarterback] Zach Mettenberger. It makes sense to have someone come down to work with the kid specifically, because it's the duty of ours to teach them how to be a pro.
>
> Now that doesn't just mean how to play pro football. It's how to be a pro on and off the field. That's part of [the development] of the player.

What's the importance of the combine in relationship to the draft?

"The higher level of football you play, the less impact it has," Linta said. "The measurables are important for lower-level guys, from Division II and III, NAIA. If you are a killer player in Division I, you have the film of what you can do and everyone has seen it in the league."

The combine has been a proving ground for many a potential pro football player—and sometimes, his downfall when players don't measure up to expectations.

The combine was first proposed by Tex Schramm, general manager of the Dallas Cowboys, as a centralized, more economical, way of evaluating talent for the NFL.

Gil Brandt, the Cowboys' top scout for three decades, was with Schramm when the GM came up with the idea of a combine.

"Prior to the 1977 draft, we were starting to bring in players for physicals," Brandt said.

The idea of a combine was sparked by a chance meeting with Nolan Cromwell. Cromwell, an All-American quarterback from the University of Kansas, showed up in Dallas for a physical.

"About 8:00 a.m., Cromwell steps off the elevator at our Dallas office," Brandt recalls. "Tex and I happen to be coming up at the same time and the player's got 10 or 12 brown envelopes under his arm. He can hardly stay awake after an overnight flight from Seattle to Dallas."

Tex looks at the sleepy, exhausted player and then at Brandt. "There has to be a better way of doing this."

And so the combine was born.

"The first combine we had took place the following spring in '78," Brandt said.

Actually, there were three different combines at first.

"We had these little combines and we brought about 150 players in," Brandt said.

The combines agreed to share physicals and any information requested.

"It was really coming in on Friday, getting examined on Saturday, go out and run a couple of 40s, do a drill and send them home on Saturday night," Brandt said. "It was a very, very limited thing."

Change was inevitable when the National Invitation Camp (NIC) was opened in Tampa, Florida, in 1982. It was originated by National Football Scouting, Inc., basically as a means to look at draft prospects and ascertain medical information on the top players.

Two other camps were opened from 1982 to 1984 before all three were consolidated into one. The NIC was then renamed the "NFL Scouting Combine" as it moved around to a variety of sites before finally finding a permanent home in Indianapolis in 1987.

The combine was first shown on TV in 2004 and has grown exponentially since then. In 2012 for the first time, the combine began airing more than 30 hours. A total of 5.24 million viewers watched the proceedings that year.

The 2014 combine was generally regarded talent-wise as one of the best ever from top to bottom.

"I've been doing this for 30 years, and this is the deepest draft that I've ever seen," said Pittsburgh Steelers general manager Kevin Colbert.

Brandt was in agreement with Colbert.

"I've been to every combine of any significance that's ever been held, and the group I saw this week in Indianapolis probably ranks among the best-conditioned crew I've seen in some time," Brandt said following the 2014 event. "Almost everybody realized this was a serious job opportunity and approached it accordingly."

Apparently, the flamboyant Deion Sanders wasn't too concerned when he made his appearance at the combine in 1989. "Prime Time" showed up late and left early after taking his turn in the 40-yard dash. Sanders ran his 40 only once, clocked a sizzling 4.19 or 4.29, depending on whose hand-time watch you believed.

Sanders was still considered one of the greatest performers at the combine and proved his worth by starring in two pro sports: football and baseball.

At first Sanders did not even want to run the 40.

"I talked him into running because I had a relationship with Deion," Brandt said. "He ran one time and that was it. In Deion's case, he was not only a football player but a baseball player. When Deion ran, he was in optimum condition."

Another two-sport athlete who made it big in the pros, but for a short span, was Bo Jackson, credited by one source in the 40-yard dash at the 1985 combine with a wicked time of 4.12.

Manziel, meanwhile, had to be the most intriguing player in the 2014 combine draft since Tim Tebow was the center of polarizing opinions in 2010.

Too short. Too unconventional. Too reckless.

That's what the critics were saying about Manziel, the kid quarterback who immodestly called himself "Johnny Football" when he was at Texas A&M. He had won the Heisman Trophy in 2012 but remained an easy target for critics because of his flashy, often reckless style of play, and his flashy lifestyle as well.

On the field with his electrifying open-field running, Manziel could be dazzling. He was so different from the conventional stay-in-the-pocket pro style, but his freelance style was perfect for college ball.

In just two years at A&M, he produced remarkable numbers: 7,820 passing yards and 63 touchdowns, and 2,169 rushing yards in just 26 starts while playing one of the toughest schedules in the nation.

Off the field, Manziel called more attention to himself but not in a positive way. Involvement with a memorabilia dealer concerning his autograph caused Manziel to be suspended for the first half of a game in 2013.

He was also investigated by the NCAA for underage drinking and had admittedly seen a counselor for the aforementioned alcohol and anger management problems.

One of the main objections by the critics was Manziel's height—5 foot 11¾—although he promised he would measure at "72 inches on the dot."

"I play with a lot of passion," Manziel told reporters at the combine. "I feel like I play 10 feet tall. A measurement to me is just a number."

Manziel could point to Seattle's Russell Wilson, another sub-six-footer who proved that size didn't matter. All he did was win a Super Bowl in February 2014.

Another area of measurement, Manziel's hands, passed with flying colors. Manziel's hands were just shy of 10 inches, larger than any other quarterback at the combine.

"All weather size," reported the *Washington Post*. "Can control ball, throwing and handling."

While Manziel was the hottest topic at the 2014 combine, some of the biggest performers were mostly unheralded, among them Kent State running back Dri Archer and Miami (Florida) punter Pat O'Donnell. Archer ran the fastest 40-yard dash, and O'Donnell put up more reps on the bench press than projected No. 1 choice Jadeveon Clowney of South Carolina.

"This is the heaviest underclass group that's come out," New England Patriots coach Bill Belichick said after the combine. "So a lot of these players weren't surprises, obviously. But because of the large numbers of them, plenty of them were."

Combine. Underwear Olympics. Call it what you will. It has been a smash hit since Schramm started things in the 1970s.

"It answers all the questions," Brandt says. "It keeps a guy from flying to 15 different cities for a physical and work out for 12 different teams."

11

THE GURUS

Guru: a master, an oracle, a sage.

NFL draft guru: a Brandt, a Kiper, a Mayock.

It wasn't until nearly a half century into the draft that the phrase "draft guru" became as much a part of the lexicon as, say, sleeper or bust. Oh, there were supposed experts, including a bunch of general managers and owners who thought they deserved such a tag.

Then they made picks such as Tom Cousineau, Ryan Leaf, or JaMarcus Russell and displayed just how much they didn't really know.

Conversely, there have been the true draft scholars, the ones who have spent most of their lives collecting the knowledge on the surefire running back from Oklahoma. And on the sacks machine from North Carolina. Or the kid from some school on the prairie with no shot at the big time who then makes it.

There are dozens, maybe even hundreds, of self-proclaimed draft experts nowadays. But four names stick out: the late Joel Buchsbaum, Gil Brandt, Mel Kiper, and Mike Mayock.

Thanks to television's infatuation with everything NFL, and particularly with the mechanisms of this springtime grab bag that helps fill pro rosters, not a day or a drive-time media slot goes by without some draft talk. Pick up a newspaper or magazine. Look at your smart phone or on your laptop or iPad. Watch the tube or listen to the radio.

You can't miss it.

"There are more and more experts out there every year," says Brandt, the personnel director for the Dallas Cowboys from 1960 to 1988 whose attachment to draft expertise covers well over 50 years. "Sometimes, all they prove is how much they don't know."

Brandt laughs at that thought, remembering how teams in the 1950s and early '60s relied on draft annuals and ratings to help in making their picks. Nowadays, that's hardly the case, with millions of dollars sunk into every team's personnel operation.

Still, the knowledge that Brandt, Kiper, and Mayock carry—and Buchsbaum certainly did before he died in 2002—might go deeper than anyone else manages.

GIL BRANDT

A onetime baby photographer whose photographic memory enables him to recall hometowns, relatives, high school coaches, and probably the IQs and GPAs of anyone he scouted, Brandt is now the league's draft consultant. Ever wonder who invites the collegians to attend the draft each year?

That's Brandt.

Ever wonder whose mock drafts, whether he posts them on nfl.com or presents them to his audience on SiriusXM NFL Radio, are usually closest to replicating what the 32 teams actually do?

That's Brandt.

"He's an NFL historian who is connected to the modern game too," says sportswriter/broadcaster Alex Marvez, who co-hosts a show with Brandt on SiriusXM. "He is a true information guy. He has all this material that is very behind-the-scenes, but he doesn't share it all, and that way has built a trust with everyone."

As the main procurer of talent for coach Tom Landry, team president Tex Schramm, and "America's Team," Brandt spent 28 years scouring the country. Consider this list of brilliant draftees that mark Brandt's tenure in Big D:

- Hall of Famers Bob Lilly, Tony Dorsett, Michael Irvin, Randy White, Rayfield Wright, Mel Renfro, Bob Hayes, and Roger Staubach—the latter three all in the 1964 Cowboys collection.
- Frequent Pro Bowler players Lee Roy Jordan, Harvey Martin, Ed "Too Tall" Jones, John Niland, George Andrie, Calvin Hill, Charlie Waters, Billy Joe DuPree, Bob Breunig, Herb Scott, and Ken Norton.
- And, not to ever be forgotten, particularly by folks in Minnesota, Dallas took running back Herschel Walker, who had starred in the United States Football League (USFL), in the fifth round in 1985. Walker not only wound up with the Cowboys but also was the prize the Vikings sought in the post-Brandt 1989 trade that became the foundation of championship teams in Dallas.

Sure, there were mistakes: 1978 second-round tight end Todd Christensen never played for the Cowboys but became a star and a Super Bowl winner with Oakland. Bill Thomas, the 1972 first-rounder, didn't start a game for Dallas and lasted only one season as a Cowboy.

"The only ones who haven't made mistakes are the ones who never make any picks," Brandt says.

Kiper calls Brandt "the trailblazer, the master of the draft. And to be doing it as long as he has been doing it. Sometimes,

Gil will say, 'OK, come over here, guru.' Then he would give me a trivia question I had no idea the answer to. But he knew. He always knew."

Nothing better displays the diligence, foresightedness, and yes, the serendipity that often accompanied Brandt's picks as the mechanisms that led to Staubach wearing the Dallas star.

Staubach went to New Mexico Military Institute (NMMI) out of high school because he didn't quite have the qualifications yet for the Naval Academy. Brandt and his staff knew the coaches at NMMI, so they got to know Staubach.

Fast-forward to the end of Staubach's playing career at Navy. Because of the relationship the team had built with Staubach, there was never any question where he would play pro ball, even though Kansas City of the AFL had also selected him in 1964.

Brandt says,

> You needed contacts that were reliable to find out what was going on. For the draft, we knew a basketball coach at Navy, Danny Peterson. We were playing in Philadelphia, too, when the draft was being held, and as soon as Army-Navy was over at the old stadium, we got Roger to the hotel and we signed him after the game to a contract.
>
> We even gave a signing bonus, kind of rolled the dice. And all the time Roger was in the service, he got that monthly stipend from us.

He got something else from the Cowboys, although his supply kept running low.

"He would write me from Da Nang [Vietnam]: 'I need more footballs.' How could he need more footballs? Well, they were in a tent and a mortar shell came in and blew them all up."

Staubach even attended Cowboys training camp one summer while he was still in the service. He stayed downtown at a hotel; Brandt recalls that Staubach was not subject to the curfews the team had, but it would never matter with such an upstanding citizen.

"Roger would go to meetings and practice with the team. You knew he was something [special]."

Indeed. After Staubach's naval commitment concluded, he joined the Cowboys in 1969 and led them to two Super Bowl titles on his way to the Pro Football Hall of Fame.

Testimonies to Brandt's brilliance not only when in the middle of the action for the Cowboys but also in his subsequent career as a journalist and draft consultant come from all directions.

Marvez marvels at Brandt's energy.

"He is relentless and still works harder than most people in this business," Marvez says. "And he has a garage full of NFL history."

Brandt has not just been a part of football history, either. He won an Emmy for a television special about the day (November 22, 1963) President John F. Kennedy was assassinated in Dallas. Marvez kids Brandt that he will someday win an Oscar and a Tony award.

Brandt is so well traveled that he's been to many of the high schools—not colleges but high schools—where future NFL players have attended. He edited the Playboy All-America team for years, which gave him extra cachet with those players.

That worldliness—Brandt once conducted a tour of Europe to find placekickers and came up with Austria's Toni Fritsch, who was with Dallas for four seasons and won a Super Bowl—also works with the draft's fan base. When someone from, say, Bozeman, Montana, asks Brandt a question, somehow the answer will include a mention of Montana State, located in that very city.

"Gil was the first personnel guy for a team to scout the traditionally black schools," Marvez notes. "He remembers those players, remembers a guy he scouted from Montana Tech. People love that, love to hear his stories."

As a tribute to his globe-trotting, one segment of Brandt's radio show has been introduced with Johnny Cash's "I've Been Everywhere."

That comfort level with the fans certainly extends to the players, Marvez says.

"At the combine, he is the guy who asks the players to come out and talk to the media. A lot of players feel comfortable with him; he has a way to reach people."

Many folks in football have called for Brandt's selection to the Hall of Fame.

As for Brandt, he's simply kept at it since Kennedy was president, Vince Lombardi was Green Bay's coach, not the name on the championship trophy, and the NFL had all of 13 teams.

JOEL BUCHSBAUM

The man Dan Arkush of *Pro Football Weekly* once called "the most astute draft tracker who ever lived" hardly seemed to fit the part of a football icon.

He wasn't well built. He wasn't even an athlete. He was hardly ever seen in the light of day.

Most often, he was unkempt. His voice came across more as a whine than as a purveyor of wisdom.

Yet during his career compiling player evaluations for the draft, Joel Buchsbaum was the man just as much as John Elway was a quarterback.

Colts general manager Ryan Grigson credited Buchsbaum for being a major influence on his career. He told Arkush,

> What I really admired about Joel was his passion. Just the eloquence of his reports, his style of writing, led me to model my own reports

after him. There was no other way for a commoner to look at a scouting report. I used to love reading his stuff. He was one of the great ones that I really looked up to because he really was a genius.

I remember checking off the names at offensive tackle the year I was drafted [1995], and he was only off one player in his book before I was picked. That just goes to show you that he really knew what he was doing.

Grigson went in the sixth round to Cincinnati, didn't make it as a player, and then went into personnel work.

Buchsbaum never got the big payoff for his brilliance. Yes, he became a household name among personnel people throughout football. Media members often called on him, and he willingly shared his expertise. His draft preview books were must reading for anyone and everyone involved with the NFL.

But the contributing editor for *Pro Football Weekly* rarely, if ever, drew the acclaim that Brandt, Kiper, and Mayock deservedly do nowadays.

Because of his quirkiness, which bordered on reclusion, Buchsbaum never had a shot—or never really gave himself a shot—at joining the mainstream. He lived alone—well, he did have pet dogs, all of them named after baseball great Brooks Robinson—in a Brooklyn apartment that, by all accounts, was dilapidated by the time he died. He spent about a month at Brooklyn College before dropping out, never to return to school.

Nor did Buchsbaum show up at the college all-star games or workouts that so many scouts attended. Games? Forget that.

He plunked himself in front of his television set, armed with hundreds, perhaps even thousands, of tapes. And that was pretty much all he did.

Bob Costas once compared meeting Buchsbaum to a sighting of Bigfoot, telling the *New York Times*, "I was never in his presence. That puts me in the same category as 99 percent of people that knew him. A portion of our audience thought he was a put-on. His voice was almost as if you invented a sports brainiac cartoon character."

Ah, but the knowledge that flowed from his mouth. Like Brandt, he had total recall of players from years before. Their strengths, their weaknesses, their 40-yard times, their injuries, their stats in college—Buchsbaum could recite them as if he was saying the Pledge of Allegiance.

He was once asked by two Associated Press football writers about a player who had just been selected in a latter round of a particular draft. Neither of the journalists knew the youngster despite doing their own thorough research of that year's crop.

Without hesitation, Buchsbaum replied crisply, "Basketball player, didn't get on the football field. Great jumper, can move laterally, smart guy. Could make it as a tight end."

The kid didn't make it, but that's not the point. Buchsbaum's immeasurable knowledge was.

Much of that knowledge rubbed off on sportswriters and broadcasters. Howard Balzer for decades has written and talked about all aspects of the NFL and is as knowledgeable as anyone about the draft; remember, he was on ESPN's initial broadcasts beginning in 1980. He recalls some classic Buchsbaum stories.

> One time, Bill Wilkerson here in St. Louis was interviewing Joel on the radio, and pretty much all the time when people mentioned Joel, they pronounced the last name "Booshbaum." That's how it looked to many people, not "Bucksbaum."
>
> So Bill introduces Joel and begins asking him questions, and Joel, in that nasal New York voice, stops him with, "BILL, BILL, IT'S PRO-NOUNCED BUCKSBAUM."
>
> And Bill, without missing a beat, says, "Joel, you have been on with us time after time and it has been Booshbaum. That's how it has been, and that's how it will remain."

Still, Buchsbaum was a regular on several radio shows for years, and though his delivery could be termed the anti–John Madden—

emotionless, often in a monotone—his information was impeccably accurate.

As for television . . .

"One time, ESPN decided to put him on TV, and it was a disaster," Balzer says. "Let's just say he was not comfortable on TV, he got very nervous. While he is on the set, I hear someone from the truck say in my ear, 'Never again.'"

That experience didn't keep Buchsbaum from helping out his TV brethren from behind the scenes. In 1982, Jeff Bryant was the first pick for Seattle, sixth overall. Balzer was sitting with noted football writer Paul Zimmerman on the ESPN set before things got started, and suddenly, Buchsbaum approaches. Off camera, naturally. Balzer says,

> I hear that voice. I hear him say, "Keep an eye on Jeff Bryant." It's Joel, looking like he hadn't slept in a week; he reminded me of Woody Allen.
>
> I leaned over and said to him to introduce myself, "Hey Joel, Howard Balzer."
>
> He looks at me and goes, "I know who you are." And he walks away.
>
> And then Seattle takes Jeff Bryant.

Two months after Buchsbaum's death on December 29, 2002, a tribute to him was held at the NFL combine. Initially, a few journalists and perhaps a scout or two were expected to attend. Instead, the place was packed with all sorts of folks associated with the NFL, including some pretty big names.

John McClain, the renowned football writer for the *Houston Chronicle*, recalled the scene to *Pro Football Weekly*.

> To see so many general managers, personnel directors and media people there was pretty unbelievable. I remember the first speaker was Bill Belichick. He had his hoodie on. He was wearing it then before he ever wore it on the sideline.
>
> I was in awe to hear him say that he twice tried to hire Joel when he was with the Browns and Patriots, and that Joel always turned

him down. I know that the Oilers also tried to hire him when Ladd Herzeg was the GM in the early '80s. They offered him $60,000. I don't know what y'all at PFW were paying him, but I know it wasn't that much.

But Joel said he felt like he'd rather work for the league and serve everybody.

McClain lamented that Buchsbaum's legacy isn't stronger with today's draftniks and believes the entire draft process has suffered since Buchsbaum passed away.

"There will never be another Joel," McClain said.

MIKE MAYOCK

Unlike Brandt, Buchsbaum, and Kiper, Mike Mayock played pro football. Not for long—a 10th-round choice of the Steelers in 1981, he wound up with the Giants for two seasons, getting into nine games as a special teamer.

A defensive back by trade, he also played baseball at Boston College and is a member of the school's Hall of Fame.

His biggest fame has come from his draft expertise—not a path Mayock planned to follow when he went into broadcasting.

How did he wind up in an industry that Brandt, Buchsbaum, and Kiper had pretty much invented but, unlike a decade later, few were aspiring to as a career in 2004?

"Because I didn't get the job I really wanted, which is highly ironic," Mayock says with a laugh.

When NFL Network started, I got an opportunity along with a bunch of big-name players to do a trial on-camera for the show that became "Total Access." I was a no-name versus these big names, and I thought I knocked it out of the park.

Howard Katz, who came from CBS to build NFL Network, called me in and said, "We will offer you a job. But it is not the job you came here for."

Mayock was stunned, almost speechless even. He wondered if he hadn't produced what the budding network was looking for in his tryout.

Katz told him the tryout was not a problem at all. Katz and other NFL Network executives had something else in mind.

"He said, 'We have to develop the college football theme and introduce our new players to our fan base. We don't know how to do it,'" Mayock says. "I got upset. I said again, 'Did I do as well or better than everyone else? Why are you relegating me to a draft show; NFL Network is not going to be about college football.'"

Actually, in part it was. Where do the future NFL players come from? What was becoming pro football's biggest off-season attraction?

Eventually, NFL Network would not only televise the draft, competing with ESPN, but also air college bowl games and all-star games live.

"Howard just said he would let me do it my way," Mayock says. "And I have."

Yes, he has. And the way Mayock does it, along with his duties as game analyst on NFL Network's Thursday-night package, plus for NBC on its Notre Dame telecasts, has drawn praise from people inside and outside the sport.

As James Brady wrote on SB Nation, "Nobody can deny that Mike Mayock is one of the most respected names among NFL draft analysts. Mayock is dedicated and possesses an encyclopedic knowledge of everything to do with the upcoming draft class. He can go on and on about this guy or that guy, regardless of position or school. Sometimes the details get ridiculous, but the man is always impressive."

Perhaps most impressive is Mayock's schedule that, apart from a vacation in July, is pretty much 24-7 football.

On August 1, he starts attending training camps, college and NFL. He's paying close attention to the draft around the entire process but is also doing preparation for his broadcasting.

"Whether I'm at Notre Dame or Michigan for their workouts, or at Patriots training camp or Raiders camp, I am still focused on the draft, too," he explains. "It is a seven-day process for me after August right up until late in the next spring."

Mayock usually gets to seven or eight NFL camps, as well as three or four college campuses, and is on the road the entire month of August.

As he rolls into September, he begins trying to catch up on tape with the rising seniors. His day can begin as early as 5:30 a.m., when the tapes are going and he's grinding on those seniors at each position. That process continues throughout the college and pro seasons.

He ignores the underclassmen, because of the uncertainty of their status.

"I have no idea who is declaring to come out or not. I get to them later when it is a sure thing [they have entered the draft]."

Throughout the season, he talks to NFL coaches, GMs, and scouts, whether on the phone or on the road. Things really pick up as far as being draft-centric in December when the college regular season has concluded and the NFL is winding down.

As soon as the NFL playoffs start in January, Mayock becomes immersed in the college all-star games. He says,

> On NFL Network we do the East-West all-star game and the Senior Bowl, and I am on the road for 15 straight days. For the East-West game, I get to Tampa for every practice because it is a chance to see lots of players who are typically the mid- to late-round guys. I get to see them work out and practice and play for four days. It's a good chance to compare notes on them, too.
>
> Then I head to Mobile, where we televise the practices live on NFL Network, and I have to know those 100 or so seniors before I

get there. So all of that intense work and [watching] tape and study-
ing these guys, it pays off at the Senior Bowl.

Mayock emphasizes to the college players that everything
is a process: the all-star games are an important step because the
people who will decide some of their futures are at those games.
They get to see firsthand how the players practice, how they
work, and their discipline. And then they see the players on the
field during a game.

Next up for the prospects is the combine, or more accurately,
getting ready for the combine. That means heading to training
centers that prime them for the drills they must conquer in Indianapolis in late February.

"Just like all the players are prepping for the combine, so am
I," Mayock says. "That's all day every day, seven days a week
trying to prepare, trying to get to know something about all 300
players. The interest in the combine has gotten so big, that's also
amazing."

NFL Network does live feeds of the combine, so Mayock
must provide data on every player who attends, even those who
don't do much more than answer questions from the media and
take psychological tests with the teams.

As soon as the combine ends, the pro days begin. With
Mayock working on the *Path to the Draft* show on NFL Network,
there's even more information he can give to the viewers in that
show.

He had to fight to get NFL Network executives' attention
when it came to pro days.

"I was pushing to go to these pro days right from the outset
with NFL Network but was told because there was no budget
for that, I could only go to two or three," he remembers. "That's
back when NFL Network got started [2004]. Now, it is, 'How
many can you get to, Mike?'"

That is usually from 10 to 15 all over the country. One year in a week's period, the itinerary was Tuesday at East Lansing for Michigan State's pro day and then on to Tuscaloosa for Alabama's on Wednesday. Then back up north to Columbus for Ohio State and then to "I forget where on Friday," he adds, laughing.

"We would either televise them live, like we did with Manziel [in 2014] at Texas A&M, or I'd provide reports from there. I get to see all the coaches and GMs and scouts at those pro days, and it helps my knowledge get better so I can give that knowledge to the fans."

Not yet totally exhausted from such a schedule, Mayock gets reenergized when April hits because, well, most years that's when the draft takes place.

He spends virtually every waking minute in April talking to teams and hearing and checking out rumors of trades, teams looking to move up and down, or medical situations.

"But what is true and is not true, let's just say there's a lot of information and a lot of *misinformation* out there," he says.

He also finds time to visit with some pro teams heading into the final days.

"And there we go—draft time."

That hectic pace and full docket is, he says, essential.

"There's quite a bit of crossover and work that is connected," Mayock says. "When I am watching NFL teams' tape, it's helping me benchmark college football players, too."

And when the draft begins, well, Mayock knows he'd better be at his peak. He doesn't worry too much about the first two nights, the three rounds, because he knows plenty about the 100 or so players who will be chosen.

"What scares the hell out of me is a name that comes up that I have never heard of in my life," he says. "That's more likely, if it happens, to be in the later rounds. Teams pick guys who never played in college—maybe basketball players or track guys. They can stump you."

Mayock doesn't shy away from relating those times he has been stumped. He says of some of them that they "really stuck in my craw" that he got it wrong.

"I totally missed on Maurice Jones-Drew," he says of the running back who came out of UCLA to Jacksonville in the second round in 2006.

> I made the assumption that because of his size he could not be an every-down back. He became a great every-down back.
>
> The big offensive tackle, [Marcus] McNeill out of Auburn. I missed there, too, in 2006, didn't think he'd amount to much in the pros. He had four or five very good years before the injuries.
>
> I also thought Blaine Gabbert [2011 first-rounder by the Jaguars] would be really good in the NFL. Looks like that one was wrong.

Pressed to balance that with some of his most accurate evaluations, when his take stood out from the others and Mayock was proven right, he points to some quarterbacks.

> JaMarcus Russell, I was at his pro day, and it was the best quarterback day I have ever seen. But at the end of it, I made the comment I wouldn't take him in the first round. I don't think it was too popular [a sentiment]. But I thought this guy doesn't love football, he showed up 20 pounds overweight at the combine. So I said, "I don't think this guy is a franchise quarterback."
>
> Jay Cutler, I thought I did a good job on him. A lot of people thought Vince Young and Matt Leinart were the best quarterbacks in that [2006] draft, and I was firmly in his corner.
>
> Same thing with Philip Rivers in '04; a lot of people thought of him as a third- or fourth-round pick coming into his senior season. He had that unusual sidearm throwing motion. Then he has a great Senior Bowl performance.
>
> I saw him as a coach's son who knew his football, got the ball out so accurately and quickly, who cares if it is sidearm? His release was one of the fastest I have seen.

With Aaron Rodgers, I took a lot of abuse for saying where I thought he would wind up. I thought he was going to slide, and not because he didn't have the talent; he was a very talented quarterback. It just seemed to me that was how the draft would go.

When the draft gets going, Mayock is on the NFL Network set at the venue, most recently Radio City Music Hall. Kiper isn't far away; they can surely see one another from their posts. Same thing for Brandt, who is working for SiriusXM NFL Radio.

To Mayock, soaking in the atmosphere is difficult because of the job requirements. But unless you have the emotions of, say, a Bill Belichick, it's impossible not to at least acknowledge the wild environment. Mayock says,

> It kind of blew me away the first time we did it at Radio City. My thinking was that it is all about football; it is really game day. It's the big game tonight. That was my approach.
>
> Then you walk into Radio City and the energy is palpable, very similar to an NFL game. When the place fills up, the energy is amazing. People are yelling and booing and cheering and wearing their team's jerseys.
>
> It's important not to get caught up too much in that. For the most part, I try to take care of my business; that's why I am there. If I am not on top of the next pick, I will be overwhelmed. We are on camera for hours . . . outside of the picks, my biggest concerns become how am I getting fed, and running to the bathroom.

Like Kiper and Brandt, Mayock admits to having a soft spot for the youngsters who attend the draft. When he sees a 10- or 12-year-old wearing a team jersey and screaming out about that club's latest pick, well, that is fandom in its most uncomplicated form.

"They are there for all the right reasons," he says, "purely as fans."

MEL KIPER JR.

Brandt worked for nearly three decades for the Cowboys. Mayock first got his taste of NFL action as a defensive back/special teamer for the Giants.

Kiper? He's a self-described "18-year-old right out of high school, looking for my life's work."

He found it, and anyone involved in the draft evaluation business can thank Kiper for bringing such endeavors to the forefront.

Kiper pretty much created the profession atop which he, Mayock, and Brandt now reign.

"No, I never thought it would happen this way. No question, the guy who developed this industry is Mel," Mayock says. "I have more respect for Mel than you can ever know; I think he kind of scouted me when I was playing."

What Kiper saw was a void in information delivery. He was already putting together a newsletter about the draft in 1978, and he drew encouragement from Ernie Accorsi, a former sportswriter who served as general manager with the Colts, Browns, and Giants.

"Ernie said that people would crave this information," Kiper recalls. "I started the business and lot of people told me that nobody was going to buy that, to get a real job; don't waste your time. They were wrong. People cared."

In the early 1980s—he didn't join ESPN's crew until 1984—Kiper was compiling draft data while living in his hometown of Baltimore. Accorsi was going to hire him for the scouting department had the Colts not abruptly moved to Indianapolis.

Kiper almost certainly would have taken that job. His reputation was building because of his thoroughness, his relentless quest for any and all information available about a pro football prospect.

He also knew that during that era, no free agency existed and there were few trades, with any major transactions extremely rare. The only real way for teams to get better was through the draft.

Because local newspapers and radio/TV tended to cover only the local teams, NFL fans didn't get much chance to see or learn about the collegians who could wind up making or breaking the future of their favorite pro club.

Kiper felt he could solve that problem. No, he *knew* he could.

"One thing to remember is that NFL fans were not big college fans then," he explains. "My reports would tie college football and the NFL together, bring their fans all together. For the college fans, you want to see where your players get drafted and what they can do. For the pro fans, you want to see how they will help your team get better."

And if those NFL followers had never heard of someone their team chose—maybe even hadn't heard of the school—Kiper knew. By his own count, he has compiled profiles of thousands of players each year, from the Alabamas and Florida States at the top level to the Grand Views and Morningsides of the National Association of Intercollegiate Athletes (NAIA).

Like Brandt and Mayock, Kiper has become a media fixture, both on radio and television. He's cohosted *College Game Day* in the past. And he doesn't stick simply with his area of expertise, either, having branched out with a regular gig on ESPN radio.

But to think that has distracted him even minutely from his true course would be folly. Just listen to this draft-centric, seven-days-a-week schedule:

In September, Kiper spends his Mondays looking at tape and gathering info on as many players as he possibly can. He also has had the opportunity to see dozens of games on satellite TV from the weekend.

He uses Monday as an evaluation day, puts together his "big board," and sends it to the folks at ESPN.

Then he's spending hours throughout the week on a variety of radio and TV shows, all the while updating his evaluations of players from the Big Ten and the Big Three, from the Southeastern Conference populated by the Auburns and Floridas to the Northeast Conference inhabited by the Sacred Hearts and Robert Morrises.

Weekends in the fall and winter, naturally, are the most frantic until players stop running with, passing, or kicking the football.

Sunday is entirely an NFL day for Kiper as he evaluates what teams have and what their holes could be. That includes breaking down NFL players' performances late that night.

"From September 1 until the draft, it is pretty much nonstop," he admits.

While Kiper has to be a huge fan of the sport to do what he does, he's never really watching games for entertainment. It's all about the info.

"You do your job, and if it is good enough, it is good enough," he says. "You can only do what you can and be who you are. It is not fun and games for me; it is business, finding the facts, and I try to give it to everyone who is interested."

By the fifth week of the season, Kiper is already getting calls from people who have lost hope in their NFL team and want to know who the top players are at every position. Seniors and juniors.

"Those are the people who already are saying, 'Let's hope we lose all our games to get the No. 1 pick.'"

Like anyone in the business of making predictions, from the local weatherman to the Kipers of the world, 100 percent accuracy is a pipe dream.

He has his regrets.

"Chris Spielman," Kiper immediately responds when asked about some not-so-charmed appraisals. "I underrated Chris; he was an overachiever at Ohio State, an All-American linebacker, won the Lombardi Award. His agent, Tom Condon, would call me and say, 'Chris puts your picture on the wall and he does 100 situps and pushups, saying, this guy I am going to prove him wrong.' He should have been a first-rounder."

Kiper also thought Andre Ware would be a big-time pro player. Ware was a flop.

Kiper was closer in the 1998 Peyton Manning versus Ryan Leaf debate, favoring Manning. But he didn't have a direct hit on what would happen with Leaf. Kiper says,

> One thing I said about Ryan, it was 50-50 on whether he would be a franchise guy. That was one thing I had right, but I didn't think he would be a bust. He had the size and the arm and did a heck of a job at Washington State.
>
> He didn't have the maturity at the time to put in the kind of work you needed, didn't live the game the way Peyton did.

Indeed, Kiper was told by then–Colts coach Jim Mora that after the draft, Peyton told him he wanted a playbook and then headed off to study it. Leaf said he was going out partying with his friends.

Among the big hits for Kiper has been Eric Swann, a semipro player with the Bay State Titans with no major college experience (he attended Wake Technical Community College in Raleigh, North Carolina). Kiper projected Swann, a powerful and quick defensive lineman who could play inside or outside, as a top 10 pick. As everyone scrambled to find footage of Swann, some prognosticators didn't have him in their top 100.

He went sixth to Arizona in 1991 and played 10 pro seasons, making two Pro Bowls.

On the other side was Illinois quarterback Jeff George in 1990. ESPN producer Fred Gaudelli had asked Kiper for a top 40 board, and with his usual comprehensiveness, Kiper compiled it.

"Mel," Gaudelli asked, "where is Jeff George?"

Kiper had George ranked 84th, a third-rounder at best.

But George had shot up all kinds of evaluation charts and was projected to go very high, possibly first overall to Indianapolis.

"We're going to put up the top 40 board and not have him on it," Gaudelli said. "Are you crazy?"

He wasn't crazy, he was Kiper-accurate. George did go at the top of the selections, and he never amounted to much more than a mediocre starter, although he lasted 12 seasons. George was 46–78 as a starter with five franchises.

Oddly, considering Kiper's early career relationship with Accorsi, the Colts were one franchise that took issue with Kiper's opinions. Certainly the most famous—infamous? comical?—incident came in 1994.

Indy had two of the first five picks and really nailed the second slot, taking Marshall Faulk, who wound up in the Hall of Fame. At No. 5, Kiper urged the Colts to grab Fresno State quarterback Trent Dilfer.

Instead, the Colts went for Nebraska linebacker Trev Alberts, and Kiper went off on the team. He said Alberts wasn't even a true outside backer, which Indy needed, and would need to make major adjustments to his game. He noted that the Colts were "picking second every year in the draft" because of such decisions, punctuating those remarks with a "Give me a break" comment.

Colts general manager Bill Tobin was furious.

"Who the hell is Mel Kiper?" he asked. "My neighbor has more credentials than Mel Kiper, and my neighbor is a postman."

Tobin also called Kiper "that jerk in Baltimore," suggesting that Kiper was carrying a vendetta against the franchise for leaving Maryland for Indiana. He said that Kiper had such a wide reach (true) that "he gets to your sister, he gets to your mother, he gets to everybody."

"He hurts people," Tobin added of the college players Kiper doesn't rate highly. "This guy can't do this, this guy is dumb."

To his credit, Kiper never went after Tobin personally.

"That whole Bill Tobin thing, Trent won a Super Bowl with Baltimore and Trev played only three seasons," he says. "It went full circle, and Trev Alberts and I wound up being friends."

Kiper also survived—and prospered—following a difficult time in 2010 when a former sports agent told *Sports Illustrated* that he had paid players while they were still in school. Several players, including Leaf, one of the biggest busts in draft history, admitted to the magazine he had received money from Josh Luchs.

Luchs cited Kiper as an aide in recruiting players to the agency of Gary Wichard, to which Kiper responded to *Sports Illustrated*, "I would never promote Gary or another agent to a player."

"Conversations with players, which are occasionally facilitated by agents, are a valuable way to get to know the players," Kiper said in a statement back then. "These conversations have never compromised my integrity, and my 32-year record supports that."

Clearly, ESPN found no reason to sanction or even dismiss Kiper, and he has remained the network's top draft expert and one of its most recognizable personalities.

He's still going strong three decades after joining the network, and when he looks over the current draft landscape, Kiper feels proud. And not a little bit vindicated.

> After thinking of all the naysayers—and now to see the thousands of people who are evaluating the draft and scouting the draft—it's great.
>
> I guess to me it is an exclamation point. I thought it would be something everyone would crave and want. It has been verification of the idea you had when you were a high school senior in 1978.

12

THREE FOR THE SHOW

ELI MANNING

Eli Manning didn't look too pleased. In fact, he looked pissed off.

His name was announced as the top overall pick in the 2004 NFL draft, but he frowned as he walked out on the stage at the Theater at Madison Square Garden in New York.

Not that he minded being the No. 1 pick. He just didn't like the team that drafted him.

So what did he do after he was selected by the San Diego Chargers? He simply forced his trade to the New York Giants.

Manning's power play was unusual for most players in the NFL, but as the No. 1 overall pick the Ole Miss quarterback had a little more leverage than most.

It had happened before in two major cases in pro football, one involving Bo Jackson and the other John Elway. Jackson, a brilliant two-sport star who was the No. 1 pick in the 1986 NFL draft, turned his back on the Tampa Bay Buccaneers to pursue a career in baseball with the Kansas City Royals. He eventually played both sports professionally, joining the Los Angeles Raiders in the NFL.

Elway said good-bye to the Baltimore Colts and hello to the Denver Broncos.

Usually at the draft the selected player walks on the stage wearing the team cap. The audience at Madison Square Garden must have known something was up when Manning appeared holding the Chargers hat. Holding it, not wearing it.

"Wear the hat!" several fans yelled.

Manning wasn't exactly thrilled either to receive the Chargers jersey with the "1" on it that had been presented to him by NFL commissioner Paul Tagliabue.

Standing with Tagliabue and his parents for a photo op, Manning didn't look like someone who had just been selected atop the entire draft.

You couldn't say the Chargers weren't warned about Manning's hard-line stance. Or, actually, the hard-line stance adopted by his father, onetime college and NFL star Archie Manning.

A prize quarterback, Archie Manning himself had been a first-round pick (No. 2 overall) in the 1970 draft by the Mannings' hometown New Orleans Saints. Archie had been an adored cult figure in his college days at Mississippi, known as "Huck Finn in shoulder pads" because of his freckled, all-American-boy look. A lot was expected of him when he joined the Saints.

"I think even my teammates must have thought I was some kind of superman," Archie Manning recalled.

By 1978, Manning reached his potential, capping the season with numerous awards, including player of the year in the NFC. In the Pro Bowl that season, Manning led a 13–7 victory for the NFC.

Manning remained in the NFL for 14 seasons, finishing with the Minnesota Vikings. Oddly enough, despite his great talent, Archie Manning never went to the playoffs or had a winning record. In later years, he became just as well known, maybe more so, for the exploits of sons Peyton and Eli.

When Peyton was the first choice by the Indianapolis Colts in the 1998 draft, Archie gave his blessing to the University of Tennessee's star quarterback.

Not so Eli.

"I wish we could have done this behind the scenes," Archie Manning said.

Instead, the Eli sweepstakes was high profile from the outset.

Archie had been in a series of meetings and conversations with the Chargers trying to work out a deal that would send Eli to another team. The Giants were among those listed by the Mannings as a possibility.

"Archie has done a lot of research on this," said Eli's agent Tom Condon, a former NFL player considered the top representative for NFL QBs. "He has talked to a lot of people around the league. And, basically, we just don't think it's a good fit for Eli [in San Diego]."

Translation: The Chargers had not had a winning season since 1995. And their record in drafting quarterbacks was nothing but poor to say the least. Among their draft goofs was taking Ryan Leaf one spot behind Peyton in 1998. Leaf became one of the draft's all-time busts.

Eli had taken on the challenge of playing at his father's alma mater at Ole Miss, once a feared program that had been struggling of late. Eli turned the downtrodden Rebels into a winner. In his senior year, he passed for 3,600 yards and 29 touchdowns and had only 10 passes intercepted. The Rebels became one of the powers in the Southeastern Conference.

But was he worth a No. 1 pick in the NFL draft? That question had to be asked, considering all the backstage maneuvering (and soap opera silliness) going on.

An hour after Eli's name was announced, he appeared at a news conference insisting that if a trade couldn't be worked out with another team he would be going to law school. Uh, huh.

And just as the glum-looking Manning was walking away from the podium, another announcement was made: Eli had been traded to the Giants.

"I'm a lot happier than I was 10 minutes ago," Manning said, then he rushed back to the main room to take a picture with a Giants cap perched on his head. Everyone was all smiles this time.

For Manning, the Giants had given up their No. 4 selection in the first round, QB Philip Rivers from North Carolina State, and three draft picks. One was a third-rounder that year, and the others their first and fifth the following year.

It was a strong draft for quarterbacks in 2004. Ben Roethlisberger of Miami in Ohio ended up going to Pittsburgh with the 11th overall choice. He was considered on a par with Manning and Rivers by many.

"We selected Eli, and we were prepared to deal with that," Chargers general manager A. J. Smith said. "When the Giants selected Philip Rivers, some dialogue took place. Let's just leave it at that. Obviously, we know how it materialized."

The trade turned out well enough for both teams but clearly in favor of the Giants: they won the Super Bowl in the 2007 season and again in 2011 with Eli Manning at quarterback.

Both times, Manning was voted Super Bowl MVP.

BO JACKSON

It's pretty much unheard of that a Heisman Trophy winner walks away from a pro football contract worth millions to play baseball at a significantly reduced salary.

But Bo Jackson, a two-sport star in the 1980s and 1990s, was one of a kind.

Following his Heisman season at Auburn in 1985, it was naturally assumed Jackson would join the NFL. In fact, Tampa Bay made Jackson the No. 1 overall pick in the 1986 draft.

Then the running back threw the Buccaneers, and everyone else, a curve.

He announced he was going to play baseball with Kansas City. The Royals had made Jackson a fourth-round pick in the Major League Baseball draft.

Growing up in Bessemer, Alabama, Jackson excelled in baseball first and then football and track. Recruited out of high school by the New York Yankees, Jackson opted to go to Auburn, where he would become a standout in all three sports.

At Auburn, Jackson rushed for 4,303 yards and 43 touchdowns over four seasons. In baseball, he batted .335 over three years, missing his sophomore year because of a dispute with the coach.

Baseball was the sport closest to his heart, he said. Not that the Buccaneers didn't pull out all stops trying to dissuade him from pursuing a career in baseball.

As the story goes, Jackson was flown into Tampa on the private jet of Bucs owner Hugh Culverhouse to work out and take a physical. He wasn't aware of the repercussions. Jackson found out later that his little trip made him ineligible to play baseball for the remainder of the college season.

Jackson was miserably unhappy, angered even more when the Bucs' owner reneged on a promise to make him the highest-paid NFL rookie in history.

Jackson made himself a promise never to play for Tampa Bay. He simply didn't like the way the organization had been run. The team had been the laughingstock of the NFL, failing to make the playoffs year after year. Among other things, Jackson complained about the Bucs' offensive line, a key for any running back's success.

The Bucs' sorry story had been downright ugly, sometimes historically so.

In a performance of stunning futility, they lost their first 26 games under John McKay, who otherwise was highly successful at the college level with Southern Cal. That included the first all-loss record in NFL annals, 0–14 in their debut season of 1976.

McKay was known for his quips. After another defeat in a dismal season for the Bucs, McKay was asked what he thought about his team's execution.

"I think it's a good idea," he fired back.

Things hadn't changed much by the time Jackson made his commitment to baseball in 1986. As far as Jackson was concerned, Tampa Bay didn't exist. He told his agent to refrain from speaking to the Bucs.

On June 20, 1986, Jackson signed a three-year contract with the Royals for $1.066 million. In doing so, he became the first Heisman Trophy winner since 1958 to turn down a pro football contract. The previous one: Army back Pete Dawkins.

In ignoring the Bucs' reported five-year deal of $7.6 million, Jackson had now fully separated himself from professional football.

His message to the media: he wouldn't miss football one bit.

"The pads? The hitting? No. I'm concentrating on baseball, baseball. Football is nowhere in the picture," he said.

The Royals' management had to love it. As Jackson continued to build his baseball career, the Royals were enjoying all the attention focused on him and a brilliant "Bo Knows" national marketing campaign by Nike in the late 1980s and early 1990s. It made him one of the most popular athletes in America.

Jackson's baseball game ranged from struggling to spectacular.

In one instance in the 1989 season, the Seattle Mariners had the quick-footed Harold Reynolds on first base. The batter hit a line drive up the left-center field gap all the way to the warning track. Reynolds was on his way home to score a run for Seattle.

Or was he?

Jackson fielded the ball cleanly and fired a strike on the fly that nipped Reynolds at home.

Later that season, Jackson was batting against Baltimore's Jeff Ballard as Ballard was delivering a pitch. Jackson tried to call a timeout. It wasn't granted, and Jackson quickly stepped back into the batter's box, just in time to hit a home run.

Then came his famous "wall run" in 1990 when he ran along almost parallel to the ground before snaring a fly ball.

The words *potential* and *power* always seemed to surround Jackson as he built his baseball career with the Royals. During the 1990 season he hit home runs in four consecutive at-bats to tie a major league record. His home runs usually weren't cheapies, either.

"Potentially, I've never seen anybody with the batting strength this kid has," Royals manager Dick Howser said. "For sheer power, he's like Mickey Mantle, Harmon Killebrew and Frank Howard. When they hit a ball, it keeps going."

There were other times for Jackson where the ball wasn't going anyplace. Still learning to hit the curve, Jackson had a habit—like many other home run hitters—of striking out. A lot.

In 1990, Jackson fanned 172 times in 561 plate appearances. That tied him for the 10th most strikeouts in a season for a right-handed batter since 1893.

After some of those strikeouts, the temperamental Jackson would snap the bat in two on his thigh or on top of his batting helmet.

Never one to stay away from controversy, Jackson found himself in the middle of a beauty when he suddenly announced he was thinking of taking up football as a "hobby" in between baseball seasons.

"Whatever comes after baseball season is a hobby for Bo Jackson just like fishing and hunting," he said, speaking in his usual third person at a news conference.

To Tampa Bay coach Ray Perkins, who had tried to recruit Bo, it was the height of arrogance.

"I think that's a pretty far-fetched statement—as an off-season hobby," Perkins said. "To me, football is a career."

Jackson's announcement drew an angry response from many of his Royals teammates.

"Some people are upset, some are behind him," said Royals third baseman George Brett. "He's opened the door for criticism whenever he goes bad."

Jackson's consideration of double duty was not unprecedented.

The most notable to play both professional football and baseball might have been Jim Thorpe, one of the greatest athletes in American history.

In 1950, Thorpe was voted the Associated Press' greatest athlete in the first half of the 20th century. Thorpe played professional football for six teams from 1920 to 1928, starting his career with the Canton Bulldogs and finishing with the Chicago Cardinals. He played baseball for the New York Giants during the First World War, as well as with two other major league teams.

A basketball player and world-class track star as well, Thorpe won two gold medals at the 1912 Olympics. But he was stripped of the gold when it was discovered he had been paid to play baseball.

Other examples of two-sport pros: Steve Filipowicz, Carroll Hardy, and Tom Brown.

In the 1940s, Filipowicz played for both baseball and football teams in New York City. Hardy, a running back in the 1950s with the San Francisco 49ers, also played for four major league teams from 1958 to 1967. In the 1960s, Brown played as a safety for the Green Bay Packers and as an outfielder/first baseman with the Washington Senators.

Before Jackson finished his baseball career, he also played for the Chicago White Sox and California Angels.

But he made good on his promise to return to the gridiron. Jackson signed with the Raiders in 1987 and spent parts of four seasons with them. In three of those years, he had the longest runs from scrimmage: 91, 92, and 88 yards.

Sadly, Jackson's athletic career was cut short by a hip injury in a January 1991 playoff game. Jackson suffered the injury early in the third quarter of the Raiders' 20–10 victory over Cincinnati when tackled at the end of a long run.

Jackson had hip-replacement surgery and considered making a comeback in baseball. Football with a new hip was out of the question.

Finally, so was baseball. He called it quits.

"Enough is enough," Jackson said. "I'm retiring."

JOHN ELWAY

It was 1983, and Baltimore sports were headed for tough times.

The problem was quarterback John Elway, who turned thumbs down on an opportunity to play for the Colts.

The Colts had made the Stanford University star the No. 1 overall pick in the NFL draft, hopeful he could resurrect a dormant franchise that once claimed John Unitas, and then Bert Jones, as its QB.

It didn't matter to the Colts that Elway had made it known he wouldn't play in Baltimore.

"I wanted to give football a chance," Elway said, "but there is no way I'm going to play in Baltimore. I told the Colts on three different occasions, but I guess they just didn't believe I would pass up the chance."

Elway had a preference to go west, young man, maybe wind up in San Diego, Los Angeles, or Seattle. Elway had another card he could toss into the game too.

"If they can't or won't trade me to a West Coast team, I'm going to sign with the Yankees."

The Yankees? Indeed, because Elway also had prospects of a baseball career, having played for the Yankees' Class A team in Oneonta.

What was wrong with playing for the Colts? He had nothing against the city, Elway said many years later, only against Colts owner Robert Irsay and coach Frank Kush.

"I said it 800 times," Elway noted several years later. "I'm at the point where I'm kind of tired of saying it because it was never anything against the city. It was Kush and Irsay. That's the whole deal."

All this noise was happening before Irsay was about to make his Big Move. Irsay had been in long and bitter talks with the city government for a new stadium in Baltimore. Negotiations had not gone well.

He was furious, ready to move his team out of town and start fresh in a new place. Irsay had been in secret negotiations with more than a few cities and finally settled on Indianapolis as the Colts' next destination.

In drama worthy of a soap opera, it was arranged in the early hours of the morning for 15 trucks to pack the team's property and hurriedly transport it to Indianapolis. As a diversion tactic, the trucks took different routes so the Maryland State Police would not be able to enforce the newly signed eminent domain law that would have forced the Colts back to Baltimore.

While Baltimore's sports fans were sulking, Indianapolis fans were rejoicing. The new team in town received 143,000 ticket requests in just two weeks.

Elway, meanwhile, had earlier taken another route to join with his own destiny. Realizing Elway meant what he said about not playing for the Colts, Irsay had traded him to the Denver Broncos for offensive lineman Chris Hinton, backup quarterback Mark Herrmann, and a first-round pick in the 1984 draft.

Elway, a huge star at Stanford, was one of the most anticipated athletes in pro football history. He went through the usual growing pains as a rookie before developing into one of the game's greats.

But even as a rookie he showed signs of leadership. As fate would have it, Elway and his Broncos came into Baltimore to face the team he had rejected. The young quarterback stayed cool despite a barrage of boos and jeers from the fans at every snap.

Elway had a mediocre game and veteran Steve DeBerg was credited with the victory, but Elway showed his mental toughness. He would show a whole lot more three months later when the Colts came to Denver.

Elway brought the Broncos back from an almost-certain defeat. The Broncos were losing 19–0 when Elway tossed three touchdown passes in the fourth quarter, lifting them to a stunning 21–19 victory. It was 1 of 47 comeback wins engineered by Elway, more than any other quarterback in league history.

In 1986 came a signature moment of his career when Elway led the Broncos to the Super Bowl. In Broncos lore it would forever be known as "The Drive."

Down seven points late in the AFC title game at Cleveland, the Broncos faced a daunting task: 98 yards to go and time running out.

In the span of 5 minutes, 2 seconds, Elway took the Broncos downfield in a spectacular clutch drive that tied the game with 37 seconds left in regulation. The Broncos won in overtime.

Bringing teams back from the edge became a trademark of Elway's performances. He eventually led the Broncos to five Super Bowl appearances, winning two of them.

Next stop: Hall of Fame.

"You talk about defining a city," said Jim Saccomano, the Broncos' director of media relations during Elway's playing career. "You can ask people in Denver where they were when they heard about the Elway trade and they can tell you. They remember it the way they remember the Kennedy assassination."

13

IRRELEVANT MEN, TALL TALES, AND SHORT STORIES

IRRELEVANT WEEK

At the NFL draft in 2014, just about everyone knew who was going to be picked No. 1: South Carolina defensive end Jadeveon Clowney, of course.

Not many had heard of Lonnie Ballentine, the Memphis strong safety.

By the time the seven-round draft was over, Ballentine was no longer anonymous. He had considerably raised his profile as "Mr. Irrelevant"—the last player selected in the draft at 256, by the Houston Texans.

That put him in a special class as the star of "Irrelevant Week," a celebration honoring the final pick in the NFL draft. Ballentine was presented with an all-expenses-paid trip to California, a parade in his honor, and a ton of gifts featuring the "Lowsman Trophy," a spoof modeled after the Heisman. This particular model features a player dropping the football instead of carrying it in the more familiar straight-arm fashion.

Irrelevant Week? Really?

Yes, really. The tradition was kicked off by Paul Salata, a former NFL player who always had a weak spot for the underdog. Headquartered in Newport Beach, Irrelevant Week raises money for charity at the yearly event. The 2014 event, the 39th Irrelevant

Week, raised money for the Special Olympics in Southern California. Salata's group has raised more than $1 million for charities.

A former NFL player, movie actor, and entrepreneur, Salata made a fortune in the construction business in Southern California's home-building boom in the 1950s and 1960s.

"I always said if I ever could afford it, I was going to do something for the guy you never heard of," Salata said.

For a while the NFL didn't care to hear anything about Irrelevant Week. It was little more than a lightly regarded stepchild of the NFL and went largely unrecognized. But now the league embraces the concept, allowing either Salata or his daughter to stand at the official podium and announce the name of the final player in the draft.

Ballentine even received a letter from NFL commissioner Roger Goodell congratulating him on his selection as Mr. Irrelevant.

"When I played, I was sort of a champion of the guy who never gets recognized," Salata said in an interview with *Sports Illustrated*.

With the Trojans in his senior year, Salata caught 50 passes to rank third in the league.

He went on to the pros, playing for a number of teams in both the All-America Football Conference (AAFC) and NFL. When the Baltimore Colts folded in 1950, he was declared draft eligible and picked up in the 10th round of the 1951 NFL draft by the Pittsburgh Steelers. He finished up his playing career in Canada.

As for Irrelevant Week, it's quite a party that Salata and associates have put on in Newport Beach since starting the event in 1976.

"We ask each Mr. Irrelevant if they can swim, because one year we had surfing and other water activities planned for Mr.

Irrelevant, but he couldn't swim," said Melanie Fitch, Salata's daughter.

Ballentine was one who could. Water sports were only one of the many activities in which Ballentine participated. Among other things, he attended a big welcoming party, learned to surf in the Pacific, sail a yacht, and drag the infield at an Angels–Blue Jays game.

Then he attended a banquet where he was roasted before an audience of 350 featuring John Robinson, the former Southern Cal and Rams coach.

"The first time I heard Newport Beach, I thought it was an old, retirement-type deal," Ballentine said. "It didn't turn out that way at all."

One other thing: Ballentine even met Mickey Mouse and got to scream that he was going to Disneyland. And he didn't have to win a Super Bowl to do it.

"I had no idea how big of a deal this was going to be," Ballentine said.

Indeed. Nor did any of the other Mr. Irrelevants.

"I looked back and it was fun," Marty Moore, a former linebacker with the New England Patriots, said of Irrelevant Week. "It was good because people remembered who I was."

His Mr. Irrelevant tag in the 1994 draft served as a launching pad for a successful eight-year tenure in the NFL. Moore, who also played in Cleveland, became the first Mr. Irrelevant to start a game as a rookie and to play in the Super Bowl. (He played in the Patriots' loss to the Packers and then won a ring in the Patriots' victory over the Rams.)

Moore was among the more successful Mr. Irrelevants since Salata got his party going. Every once in a while a player chosen Mr. Irrelevant will surprise you.

Take placekicker Ryan Succop, for instance. The Kansas City Chiefs did. The last player picked in the 2009 draft from the University of South Carolina, Succop literally got off on the right foot by tying an NFL record by completing 86.2 percent of his kicks.

At the end of the 2011 season, Succop signed a five-year contract extension. In 2012 he became the Chiefs' all-time leader in field goals attempted and field goals made in a game, going 6 for 6 on the way to an overtime victory over the New Orleans Saints.

It was the second time the Chiefs got lucky with the final pick of the draft. It had happened earlier in 1978 when they selected quarterback Bill Kenney with the 333rd pick from the University of Northern Colorado. Kenney played a good portion of his nine-year football career as the Chiefs' starting quarterback. Kenney's best year came in 1983 when he set a club record with 4,348 passing yards and was selected for the Pro Bowl.

Two other Mr. Irrelevants who became relevant: David Vobora and Jim Finn. Vobora became a starting linebacker as a rookie with the St. Louis Rams, Finn played fullback for the Indianapolis Colts and New York Giants. For trivia fans, Finn played in the same backfield as the Manning brothers (Peyton with the Colts from 2000 to 2002 and Eli with the Giants from 2003 to 2006).

Like many others, Finn just enjoyed playing along with the Mr. Irrelevant concepts in zany celebrations that have featured a tournament where golfers try to find their balls in a sea of marshmallows.

"At first it looked like mockery," noted Finn of the celebration, "but once you're there, you kind of relax, settle in, and see it's all in good fun."

That's exactly how Lonnie Ballentine felt, once he got into the spirit of things.

"I had a fifth- or sixth-round grade and then when it didn't work out that way I had some doubts in my mind about being drafted," Ballentine said. "A lot of guys don't get drafted, so it's a blessing to say I'm one of the best 256 players this year."

NO KIDDING

When Lonnie Ballentine was named "Mr. Irrelevant" as the last pick in the 2014 draft, he received a congratulatory letter from NFL commissioner Roger Goodell. The commish showed a lighter side of himself.

Goodell wrote that Ballentine had a good chance of making the Houston Texans "if you can survive Irrelevant Week."

Looking Like $15 Million

During his time at Irrelevant Week, Ballentine was roasted at a banquet of 350 guests featuring some of sports' most notable personalities. John Robinson, the former Southern Cal coach, was the roast-master.

Mike Haynes, the Hall of Fame cornerback, was also in attendance along with noted agent Leigh Steinberg. Steinberg not only spoke but also handed Ballentine a $15 million check.

Ballentine reacted to Steinberg with a shocked look: you're kidding, right?

He was.

"That is good for at least tonight," Steinberg said.

Just one of the many hijinks that went on during the week.

That's Salata Catches

When he played football at Southern Cal, Paul Salata likes to joke that he led the league in skipped classes and scalped tickets.

He failed to mention that one season, his 50 receptions were third best in the league.

"Of course, we counted my catches in practice, warm-ups, and at halftime," Salata said.

Crowded

Talk about going deep, Kelvin Kirk was the last player picked in 1976 in a draft year when more players were picked by NFL teams than any other. That year, 486 players were picked before Kirk, a wide receiver from Dayton, was taken by the Pittsburgh Steelers. That year there were 28 rounds.

Not Wide Enough

Though he didn't play college football, track star Carl Lewis was drafted by a National Football League team. The Dallas Cowboys figured, with his speed, Lewis could be a great wide receiver in the pros. So the Cowboys took Lewis in the 12th round of the 1984 draft, 334th overall. To no avail. Lewis never played in the NFL.

Out of Sight

The "Mr. Irrelevant" award of the 2005 NFL draft went to tight end Andy Stokes of little-known William Penn University in Oskaloosa, Iowa. He remained out of touch when a reporter tried to reach him.

No response to the telephone message.

"[It created] a pinnacle of a reporter's career: getting ignored by Mr. Irrelevant," the reporter quipped.

Pat on the Back

Not many seventh-round picks in the NFL draft get to make a success of it in the pros. A rare exception was Marty Moore, selected by the New England Patriots in 1994.

Moore worked so hard in rookie camp he won the affection of his teammates. So much so that he earned a new nickname other than Mr. Irrelevant.

Now he was sarcastically dubbed "Mr. Insignificant" by his fun-loving teammates.

Forever Young

Bobby Beathard and George Young were pals but also huge rivals as general managers, Beathard mostly with the Miami Dolphins and the Washington Redskins and Young with the New York Giants.

One year the NFL draft went from 8:00 a.m. to 3:00 a.m. for 12 rounds because of the fiery competition the league was getting from the upstart United States Football League.

About 2:00 a.m., the phone rings at the Associated Press office in New York. On the phone was college football writer Herschel Nissenson, calling from the draft site. Nissenson said he had looked through every bit of information he had but couldn't find the player the Giants had drafted.

"It was a cornerback named Al Moore or something from Virginia Tech," said Paul Montella, who had fielded the call from Nissenson. "Not in the media guide. Nowhere."

Then Nissenson checked the basketball guide.

"Sure enough, Al was the point guard. Turns out, he had been an all-state high school football player in North Carolina" but never played football in college.

Young found out that Beathard had a guy stationed at the player's dorm to sign him as a free agent as soon as the draft ended. So George liked him and took him. Never got out of camp.

SHORT STORIES

Shuffle off to Buffalo

In the NFL, good friendships can only go so far.

Dick Vermeil would tell the story about the time he was coaching the Philadelphia Eagles, and he had a good relationship with Chuck Knox, who was then coaching in Buffalo. The Eagles loved Perry Tuttle, a wide receiver out of Clemson, and Vermeil told Knox they had their eye on Tuttle.

In the 1982 draft, the Bills were two or three picks behind the Eagles in the first round, and out of nowhere the Bills traded in front of the Eagles to take Tuttle. Vermeil always said after that, "It shows there are no friends around the draft."

The irony was that the Eagles took Mike Quick, who became one of their best players, and Tuttle didn't amount to much in Buffalo.

Drafty Maneuvering

Sometimes you win, sometimes you lose, and sometimes things just fall right into place. Ask Gil Brandt, who helped to build the Dallas Cowboys into "America's Team" with his smart draft picks. Brandt recalled,

> In 1963, for the '64 draft, we were in Chicago and I had talked to Paul Warfield, who was such a great player at Ohio State, and he

was going to be our first choice. Dante Lavelli was sitting with him, because this was during the war with the American Football League and there was a battle for players. Dante's instructions were as soon as we draft him, you sign him.

In the morning, I get a call from [Cowboys coach] Tom Landry. He says, "Tex [Schramm] and I decided to trade our first pick to Pittsburgh for Buddy Dial. We need a veteran wide receiver."

The Cowboys completed the deal.

Dial played three seasons for Dallas and had only two TD receptions and 42 catches for the Cowboys.

Warfield went on to a Hall of Fame career, playing for Cleveland and Miami. Brandt continues,

> One thing else to remember about that draft: Tom had already left, with Tex and me there at one of the 14 tables. We drafted Bob Hayes about 10 o'clock at night; the guy drafted after that was Bill Parcells. About midnight, we drafted [Roger] Staubach.
>
> That's three Hall of Famers from one draft, even though we didn't get Warfield.

Almost Perfect

Bust picks? The Cowboys didn't have many when Gil Brandt was overseeing draft operations. Brandt says,

> In 1982 we had Rod Hill from Kentucky State, a kid from Detroit. Took him 25th [overall]. He was a great athlete but wouldn't hit anybody.
>
> We traded him to Buffalo, and he didn't play long there. Then he went to Canada, and in seven years in Canada he had something like 49 interceptions.

The Cowboys did have some great free agents. Brandt continues,

> One of them never played a game of college football, Cornell Green. I went to sign him March 4, 1962—the Utah State basketball season

had ended. You know, John Ralston and LaDell Anderson were coaches there at Utah State.

We met at LaDell's house. I offered him $250 to sign. He said, "You know, Mr. Brandt, I was looking for a lot more than that."

So that was that, but I figured I would ask him what is a lot more? He said, "$500."

It didn't sound like a lot more to me, and he became a great player for us, went to five Pro Bowls.

A Boastful Bosworth

One of Bo Jackson's most notable performances in his rookie year came on *Monday Night Football* against the Seattle Seahawks, week 11 of the 1987 season.

At a media event before the game, Seattle's star linebacker Brian Bosworth insulted Jackson and promised that he would easily contain him.

No problem—for Jackson, that is. The Los Angeles Raiders' running back responded by running over Bosworth near the goal line for a touchdown. Jackson later made a 91-yard run for another touchdown. This time, nobody touched Jackson as he raced down the sidelines.

At the end of the run, Jackson was racing so fast that his momentum carried him into the tunnel leading to the locker room.

Along with his two touchdowns, Jackson chalked up 221 rushing yards, at the time a *Monday Night Football* record.

Bosworth didn't have much to say after that.

The Royal Treatment

While the world waited, Bo Jackson took his time before announcing what sport he would be playing professionally—baseball or football.

Finally Jackson ended all the suspense with the announcement: Bo had signed to play baseball for the Kansas City Royals, letting down the Tampa Bay Buccaneers, who had selected him No. 1 overall in the 1986 NFL draft.

One sportswriter came up with a clever headline possibility: "Bo Shafts Bucs Royally."

Smiling Through

Tampa Bay Bucs owner Hugh Culverhouse had a memorable press conference after allowing the rights to Bo Jackson expire without compensation in 1987.

What were the Bucs going to do now? a reporter asked Culverhouse.

He thought a while and then evoked one of his favorite singers, Dionne Warwick.

"Keep smilin', keep shining, that's what friends are for."

Right Sport, Wrong Team

Decisions. Decisions.

At the 1983 NFL draft, the Baltimore Colts selected Stanford quarterback John Elway No. 1 overall.

But Elway made it clear he didn't want to play for the Colts. Owner Robert Irsay was making plans to trade his rights to another NFL team. He was talking to the New England Patriots about a possible deal featuring Pro Bowl guard John Hannah and a No. 1 pick. Other teams were also interested.

Irsay called in coach Frank Kush to ask him about the trade with the Patriots. Kush said he liked it. General manager Ernie Accorsi, on the other hand, objected.

"If you make that trade, we'll have two press conferences," Accorsi said. "The first to announce the trade, and the second to announce my resignation."

Irsay backed off, and Accorsi drafted Elway even though he was threatening to play baseball instead of playing for the Colts.

Accorsi had good reason to think that Elway's baseball career was a bluff. The Colts' GM had a baseball scouting report that opined he was not a top prospect. He would be far better off as a professional football player. Accorsi thought if the Colts hung in, Elway would eventually sign with them.

As it turned out, Accorsi was right—baseball was just a bluff. But he guessed wrong on which team Elway would play for—it was the NFL's Denver Broncos.

Drafty

It was the 1983 NFL draft, and the Baltimore Colts' marketing director, Bob Leffler, was making plans to hold a party at the Baltimore Convention Center.

John Elway was far and away the best player in the draft. Leffler, and many others, never dreamed the Colts wouldn't make him the top overall pick.

There was plenty of excitement at the center, featuring a satellite dish to broadcast the event on ESPN and live commentary for the fans from Mel Kiper Jr. Leffler even had a mannequin dressed up to look like Elway.

Then Elway came on TV and said he wouldn't play for the Colts.

"I felt pretty foolish," Leffler said.

Sammy and Sid

With their amazing passing ability, Sammy Baugh and Sid Luckman were both credited with opening up the aerial game in pro football in the 1930s and 1940s.

With Baugh drafted No. 6 in 1937 by the Washington Redskins and Luckman No. 2 overall by the Chicago Bears in 1939, a lot was expected from both players. They didn't disappoint, as Luckman won four league championships and Baugh two.

They set marks that still remain among the top all time.

Baugh completed 70.3 percent of his passes in 1945, second highest all time. Sixty years after Luckman first suited up for the Bears, he remained the team's all-time leading passer at a near 60 percent completion rate.

Lots of Luck

The 1940 NFL championship game featured Sammy Baugh and Sid Luckman, two of the all-time quarterback greats. Only this time, the usually reliable Baugh wasn't so great.

Luckman's Chicago Bears walloped Baugh's Washington Redskins 73–0 in the most lopsided championship game in NFL history.

The Redskins had defeated the Bears 7–3 on the same Griffith Stadium field in Washington three weeks earlier. This time, the Redskins botched a scoring opportunity early in the game when Washington receiver Charlie Malone dropped a pass from Baugh on the goal line. At the time, the Bears had only scored seven points and the issue was still in doubt.

After the game, a reporter approached Baugh and asked him if he thought the game would have been a different story had Malone not dropped that pass.

"Sure," Baugh said, responding with a smirk, "the final score would have been 73–6."

King for a Day

In the 1940s, Hollywood and football players went hand in hand.

A number of serials, many of them 12 episodes, were turned out using football stars as leading men.

Sammy Baugh was part of that trend, playing the role of a college football star named Tom King for the Republic serial that battles Nazi-like saboteurs.

"Baugh is no threat to [Laurence] Olivier, but athletically, he's perfect for the role of the ever-charging lawman," wrote the *San Francisco Chronicle* in 1992.

Player of the Century

Clarence "Ace" Parker didn't think he belonged in the Pro Football Hall of Fame. "I always thought I was too small," Parker said upon his induction into the hall in Canton, Ohio, in 1972. "I weighed 168 pounds and was five feet ten inches tall. So I couldn't compare to the others. I thought I would be passed over. Since I was selected I want to say that I'm sure glad it happened while I'm still here."

The onetime ace of New York City football in the 1940s was a second-round draft choice out of Duke by the Brooklyn Dodgers in 1937.

Parker stood tall among his teammates. In 1940 he won the NFL's top player award for his all-around work as a quarterback, defensive back, and punter. The competition in the league was pretty stiff at that time, featuring Sammy Baugh and Sid Luckman.

Parker's legacy would later feature a unique distinction that no other Pro Football Hall of Fame member could claim: he was the only member of the hall to reach the 100-year mark.

He died in 2013 at the age of 101.

Frankie and Sammy

Before Frank Filchock was involved in a gambling scandal in the mid-1940s, the quarterback/running back had quite a football career going in the NFL.

In the 1938 NFL draft, Filchock was the second pick of the Pittsburgh Pirates (now the Pittsburgh Steelers). One year later, Filchock was sold to the Washington Redskins, sharing quarterback duties with Sammy Baugh.

While alternating with Baugh, Filchock actually managed to win the league's passing championship in 1939 and 1944.

Filchock would eventually give up his football uniform for a navy uniform during the Second World War. It was at the end of the war that Filchock got involved in a gambling scandal featuring his New York Giants team. Filchock went to Canada to finish up his football career.

But while Filchock was teaming with Baugh, the pair were two of the best backs on any one team in the NFL. The two were so popular they were tagged by the media: "Slingin' Sam and Flingin' Frank."

14

MOCK DRAFTS

From the day after the NFL draft until moments before the next one, mock drafts are being written, posted, broadcast—whatever.

They have become as common in pro football as the bracket pools are for the NCAA basketball tournament. And just like trying to predict the Final Four teams, it's nothing more than an exercise in guesswork.

So here's a look at the Associated Press's (AP) mock draft for 2014 (which did not include trades), with the actual pick underneath the AP's choice. And below that, your very own mock draft list, for use whenever.

Enjoy.

1. Houston (2–14)
Despite flopping from AFC South power to worst in league, Texans aren't that far away talentwise. New coach Bill O'Brien gets a good start on rebuilding with best overall player.
   JADEVEON CLOWNEY, DE, SOUTH CAROLINA
   CLOWNEY
2. St. Louis, from Washington (7–9)
Rams wouldn't mind trading out of here, a pick they got in the 2012 Robert Griffin III deal. If they keep it, they get different kind of RG: road grader.

GREG ROBINSON, OT, AUBURN
ROBINSON

3. Jacksonville (4–12)

Gus Bradley has cut his teeth as defensive master. Now he gets fierce pass rusher who could go at linebacker or end.

KHALIL MACK, LB-DE, BUFFALO
BLAKE BORTLES, QB, CENTRAL FLORIDA

4. Cleveland (4–12)

If new front office regime makes this pick, it will make sense. If owner Jimmy Haslam insists on high-profile QB with Heisman Trophy in his collection, all bets are off.

SAMMY WATKINS, WR, CLEMSON
BUFFALO ACQUIRED PICK, SELECTED WATKINS

5. Oakland (4–12)

Having acquired Matt Schaub from Houston, QB issues no longer are front and center in Oakland. Except that these are the Raiders, so . . .

JOHNNY MANZIEL, QB, TEXAS A&M
KHALIL MACK, LB-DE, BUFFALO

6. Atlanta (4–12)

Falcons badly need some protection for QB Matt Ryan, and there still are two ready-for-prime-time blockers available. They take one with NFL bloodlines.

JAKE MATTHEWS, OT, TEXAS A&M
MATTHEWS

7. Tampa Bay (4–12)

Sometimes by now, there's a falloff in talent from the very elite. Not in this draft, so Bucs help passing game with yet another Aggie.

MIKE EVANS, WR, TEXAS A&M
EVANS

8. Minnesota (5–10–1)

Vikings will be tempted to add young quarterback, but with Christian Ponder flop still fresh in their minds, they go defense.

> ANTHONY BARR, LB, UCLA
>
> CLEVELAND ACQUIRED PICK, SELECTED JUSTIN GILBERT, CB, OKLAHOMA STATE

9. Buffalo (6–10)

Bills were hoping for Evans, also will consider other wideouts from deep class and then opt for just what coach Doug Marrone likes most: a rugged offensive lineman.

> TAYLOR LEWAN, OT, MICHIGAN
>
> MINNESOTA ACQUIRED PICK, SELECTED ANTHONY BARR, LB, UCLA

10. Detroit (7–9)

Cornerback or safety to deal with Aaron Rodgers and Jay Cutler four times a season? If Lions stay put, they have choice of best at either position.

> JUSTIN GILBERT, CB, OKLAHOMA STATE
>
> ERIC EBRON, TE, NORTH CAROLINA

11. Tennessee (7–9)

Needing playmaker in secondary, best safety in this draft, from a winning program no less, is available.

> HA HA CLINTON-DIX, S, ALABAMA
>
> TAYLOR LEWAN, OT, MICHIGAN

12. New York Giants (7–9)

With fans chanting for receiver or tight end, Giants do what they so often have done in the last two decades: bolster defense with a stud.

> AARON DONALD, DT, PITTSBURGH
>
> ODELL BECKHAM JR., WR, LSU

13. St. Louis (7–9)

Having added Robinson to trenches, Rams boost receiving corps once again—they took speedy Tavon Austin in first round last year.

ODELL BECKHAM JR., WR, LSU
AARON DONALD, DT, PITTSBURGH

14. Chicago (8–8)

Bears coveted Donald and also had their eyes on Gilbert. But there's another topnotch defensive back left, and they grab him.

DARQUEZE DENNARD, CB, MICHIGAN STATE
KYLE FULLER, CB, VIRGINIA TECH

15. Pittsburgh (8–8)

An aging team that needs a highly successful draft, Steelers concentrate on defense early and bolster linebacking corps.

C. J. MOSLEY, LB, ALABAMA
RYAN SHAZIER, LB, OHIO STATE

16. Dallas (8–8)

Cowboys have look of last-place team, especially on defense. Time to work on that area with a pass rusher.

TIM JERNIGAN, DT, FLORIDA STATE
ZACH MARTIN, G, NOTRE DAME

17. Baltimore (8–8)

Baltimore's offensive line has been inconsistent, but with top three tackles gone, GM Ozzie Newsome has to decide if a guard is worth this spot.

ZACK MARTIN, G, NOTRE DAME
C. J. MOSLEY, LB, ALABAMA

18. New York Jets (8–8)

Jets didn't expect best tight end in class to be on board, so they switch from defensive back considerations and grab . . .

ERIC EBRON, TE, NORTH CAROLINA
CALVIN PRYOR, S, LOUISVLLE

19. Miami (8–8)

Offensive line was mess even without bullying scandal. Ravens took guy Miami really sought, so Dolphins move on to
. . .

XAVIER SU'A-FILO, G, UCLA

JA'JUAN JAMES, OT, TENNESSEE

20. Arizona (10–6)

Carson Palmer's heir, someone just as tall and solidly built, becomes second quarterback chosen.

BLAKE BORTLES, QB, CENTRAL FLORIDA

NEW ORLEANS ACQUIRED PICK, SELECTED BRANDIN COOKS, WR, OREGON STATE

21. Green Bay (8–7–1)

The way Clay Matthews keeps getting nicked, Packers need another playmaker at linebacker. They have other defensive needs, too, with LB first spot addressed.

RYAN SHAZIER, LB, OHIO STATE

HA HA CLINTON-DIX, S, ALABAMA

22. Philadelphia (10–6)

Chip Kelly's speed-em-up offense gets another product from Beaver state, although not from his former team in Eugene.

BRANDIN COOKS, WR, OREGON STATE

CLEVELAND ACQUIRED PICK, SELECTED JOHNNY MANZIEL, QB, TEXAS A&M

23. Kansas City (11–5)

Chiefs must decide whether to address offensive line or receiver. Believing they can get good wideout later on, they go for . . .

CYRUS KOUANDJIO, G-T, ALABAMA

DEE FORD, DE, AUBURN

24. Cincinnati (11–5)

Michael Johnson left for Tampa, Geno Atkins comes off major injury, and one of top talents remaining happens to play D-line.

KONY EARLY, DE, MISSOURI

DARQUEZE DENNARD, CB, MICHIGAN STATE

25. San Diego (9–7)

Cornerback with decent size, good athletic ability and strong coverage skills would help San Diego match up better with Peyton Manning.

KYLE FULLER, CB, VIRGINIA TECH

JASON VERRETT, CB, TCU

26. Cleveland, from Indianapolis (4–12)

Now Browns grab that "quarterback of the future."

TEDDY BRIDGEWATER, QB, LOUISVILLE

PHILADELPHIA ACQUIRED PICK, SELECTED MARCUS SMITH, LB, LOUISVILLE

27. New Orleans (11–5)

Coordinator Rob Ryan wants difference maker on defense. Head coach Sean Payton is an offense-trained guy. Guess who wins.

MARQISE LEE, WR, SOUTHERN CALIFORNIA

ARIZONA ACQUIRED PICK, SELECTED DEONE BUCCANON, S, WASHINGTON STATE

28. Carolina (12–4)

Panthers sigh big-time when Lee goes off the board and then fill one of voids on offensive line with Jordan Gross retiring.

MORGAN MOSES, OT, VIRGINIA

KELVIN BENJAMIN, WR, FLORIDA STATE

29. New England (12–4)

So you think Bill Belichick is ready to draft and groom someone to replace Tom Brady. We don't. Not yet.

DEE FORD, DE, AUBURN

DOMINIQUE EASLEY, DE, FLORIDA

30. San Francisco (12–4)

Best player on board comes into action here.

CALVIN PRYOR, S, LOUISVILLE

JIMMIE WARD, S, NORTHERN ILLINOIS

31. Denver (13–3)

Broncos need to address offensive line for as long as Manning remains the quarterback. But dropoff there is too severe, so they also go for best player available.

LOUIS NIX, DT, NOTRE DAME

BRADLEY ROBY, CB, OHIO STATE

32. Seattle (13–3)

Pity Seahawks for having to pick last? Not quite, because they fill major hole with . . .

KELVIN BENJAMIN, WR, FLORIDA STATE

MINNESOTA ACQUIRED PICK, SELECTED BRIDGEWATER

NO.	TEAM	PLAYER	POSITION	SCHOOL
1				
2				
3				
4				
5				
6				
7				
8				
9				
10				
11				
12				
13				
14				
15				
16				
17				
18				
19				
20				
21				
22				
23				
24				
25				
26				
27				
28				
29				
30				
31				
32				